THE HAPPY BRICKLAYER

A brick-by-brick guide to building your dream life

Mark Bayer

SUMMARY

At 40 years old, I was stuck.

I'd been trapped in a job I didn't like for 25 years. I yearned for a life with a sense of purpose, and I spent years searching for an answer.

Well, I found one. One day I took a leap of faith which brought me toward achieving my dream of a happy and contented life. These days, I feel like Fräulein Maria, waltzing across a mountaintop, singing "The Hills Are Alive with the Sound of Music!"

In this book I will explain how I built my dream life, brick by brick, and I now feel as delighted as a barefoot Austrian nanny in the hilltops. I've included every step I took, and detailed what held me back for so long. You'll learn exactly just how easy it is to design your own dream life, whilst avoiding the many pitfalls along the way.

So, if you feel like there is something missing in your life and you don't want to waste another day, your first step to living your dream starts HERE.

Just remember: if a bricklayer can find happiness, so can you!

TABLE OF CONTENTS

SUMMARY 2

PREFACE 6

1. **CAREER CHOICE** 10
   BRICK ONE: Taking Stock of Where You Are Now 16

2. **YOUR LIFE IS A MANIFESTATION OF THE THOUGHTS IN YOUR HEAD** 19
   BRICK TWO: Re-Imagining Your Current Job 24

3. **THE LAW OF ATTRACTION** 28
   BRICK THREE: Setting Your Sights On A New Path 30

4. **LIFE COACHING** 33
   BRICK FOUR: Who Are You, Anyway? 39

5. **FEAR OF FAILURE** 47
   BRICK FIVE: A Brick-By-Brick Plan to Build A Better Life 54

6. **MAKING A CHANGE** 65
   BRICK SIX: Examining Your Strengths 72

7. **THE GRASS ISN'T ALWAYS GREENER** 75
   BRICK SEVEN: Setting Aside the Distractions 79

8. **A SENSE OF PURPOSE** 81
   BRICK EIGHT: Finding Your Sense of Purpose 85

9. **HYPNOTHERAPY** **89**
   BRICK NINE: Changing Your Mind 96

10. **GETTING HELP**.. **99**
    BRICK TEN: Breaking Bad Habits 110

11. **THE TV DIET** **114**
    BRICK ELEVEN: Finding The Time 119

12. **OUR BELIEF SYSTEMS ARE LEARNED IN OUR CHILDHOODS** .**121**
    BRICK TWELVE: Bad Habits Are Learned Early................. 132

13. **MONEY** **135**
    BRICK THIRTEEN: Money, Money, Money! 138

14. **MASONRY TECHNICIAN** **141**
    BRICK FOURTEEN: Take A Look In The Mirror 151

15. **TIMELINE** **154**
    BRICK FIFTEEN: Mapping Out Your Dream 159

16. **PROCRASTINATION** **162**
    BRICK SIXTEEN: Do It Today, Not Tomorrow 167

17. **COMMUNICATION** **170**
    BRICK SEVENTEEN: The People Around You 177

18. **WORK BALANCE** **180**
    BRICK EIGHTEEN: Only So Many Hours In a Day 184

19. **INSPIRING OTHERS** **187**
    BRICK NINETEEN: Finding Inspiration 194

20. **MULTISKILLED** **197**
    BRICK TWENTY: FINDING YOUR BEST BALANCE 201

21. **CHAIN REACTION** **204**
    BRICK TWENTY-ONE: THE SNOWBALL EFFECT 210

22. **SELF-HELP RESOURCES** **212**
    MANIFESTING 213
    MEDITATION 214
    BREATHING 214
    COLD WATER THERAPY 215
    YOGA 216
    PHYSICAL ACTIVITY 217
    NUTRITION 219
    THERAPY 220
    SLEEP 221
    BRICK TWENTY-TWO: HELP ALONG THE WAY 224

23. **WHAT'S HOLDING YOU BACK** **228**
    BRICK TWENTY-THREE: START ALREADY! 232

24. **THE BRICKLAYER'S BLUEPRINT FOR SUCCESS** **236**

PREFACE

Bricklaying is one of the most repetitive jobs there is. It's an endless loop you can't escape: you repeat the same task over and over, again and again, every minute of every work day. So if you're disillusioned with your job and unsatisfied with your life, I get it! That WAS me. It took me over 25 years to finally work it out—and I can help you get there too.

Our jobs take up the majority of our time and we have to fit everything else in around them. So if we're not enjoying our work, it's bound to negatively impact other areas of our lives. But there is a solution.

My only qualification to advise others on how to improve their lives is my own lived experience. I'm not a psychologist or a therapist, but I can share with you the tools I've picked up over the decades I've spent searching for a better life.

I'm naturally a good listener, and I tend to be the person all my friends call for advice, or just to offload their problems. I also think my creativity helps. When friends tell me about their difficulties, I frequently offer suggestions or solutions that my mates haven't even thought of. I love to see their faces when their minds flood with new possibilities, and I can practically hear them thinking: *How can a bloke who spends all day bending over and exposing his butt crack to the world have the answer?*

The Happy Bricklayer
Mark Bayer

In today's world, life is busy. We all feel a responsibility to provide for our families, and we tend to put our own happiness last. But how long should you force yourself to live a life that denies you the feeling of waking up excited about your day? When you were a child you were excited about the future and the opportunities that lay ahead—why not now?

In this book I will outline exactly how to design your ultimate life and how to avoid some of the pitfalls I encountered. If you follow my example and apply the same strategies, you CAN begin to live your best life. Just imagine waking up excited about your day, no longer dreading the alarm clock, and feeling energetic and positive about your job because it satisfies your sense of purpose! Then imagine returning home to your loved ones at the end of the day, totally focused on them, and not needing alcohol or junk food treats to give you a sense of false joy. Sounds pretty sweet, doesn't it?

There are two reasons I'm sharing my story of success with you here. Firstly, writing is my passion. I feel alive when I write, scratching that creative itch and feeling that I'm doing what I was born to do. The second reason is to help others. It took me an awfully long time to find happiness, hopefully when you hear my story, you won't have to wait so long to make changes in your life and start waking up happy every day.

The Happy Bricklayer
Mark Bayer

Over the years, I've spoken with dozens upon dozens of adults who can't stand their jobs. They all feel frustrated, but they think they have no other option but to keep on doing what they're doing. It tends to be the biggest issue that prevents people from being happy and content. But the truth is that you DO have options. I know it's possible because I've done it.

I believe our human minds are too creative to be boxed in with repetitive tasks, and we all crave a sense of purpose. But some jobs lack variety. Some jobs make us work way too many hours, which burns us out and makes us depressed. Overall, the challenge is to find a career we enjoy, and then—guess what? Work stops being a chore.

When you have a job that satisfies you, everything in your life improves. You don't stay up late at night because you're delaying the inevitable alarm clock. You get to bed on time so you're refreshed the next morning, because you want to be at your best. You don't need to seek out an endorphin hit from junk food or alcohol, as you're already on a high! All your relationships improve as you become your best self, and your friends and family will be drawn to this positive new you. Your health will improve because you kicked those bad habits, and you'll have more energy for exercise.

By changing your career and working in your dream job, the cycle of unhappiness will end and every aspect of your life will

The Happy Bricklayer
Mark Bayer

improve. I know because I achieved it, and every day feels like I won the lottery—because I'm doing exactly what I *would* be doing, even if I didn't have to earn a living.

There isn't any one secret that's worked for me. I've read loads of books on self-improvement and gained a little knowledge from each one. I've completed courses on life coaching and hypnotherapy: they gave me great tools as well. I've been to psychologists and a hypnotherapist, and I've chatted to dozens of people about satisfying work over the past few decades. Eventually I had to take a leap of faith, believe in myself, and go for it.

I did have to make some sacrifices. Chasing my dreams cost money, and I took some financial hits. Then there's the mental anguish of feeling like you're selfish and not adequately providing for your family. But when you achieve your dream, your family will love seeing you happier—and believe me, that makes it all worthwhile.

Throughout this book I will detail every step I took towards living my dream life, and by the end you will have all the tools you need to build your own happiness, just like a bent-over bricklayer—brick-by-brick!

1. Career Choice

I was 40 years old and I hated my job. How did that happen? When I was a kid I dreamed of being successful. But what did I want to *do*, exactly? I don't think I ever really knew. How can you make choices as a child when you have no real idea what adult life is like?

By the last few years of high school, you're expected to choose subjects that will place you on the path to your chosen career. But like most kids, at 15 I had NO idea what I was going to do for a job—I was only thinking as far ahead as the weekend! It seems only yesterday when one Sunday afternoon my dad asked me what university course I intended to do the following year. I was about two weeks into my final year of high school, and university was the LAST thing on my mind.

"University? No way, I hate school! I'm not signing up for four more years of that."

Now, these sorts of conversations didn't happen often with my dad. He was a practical man, and when he heard that he asked me what I would be doing after high school, if not university.

I said, "No idea."

The Happy Bricklayer
Mark Bayer

"No son of mine will be unemployed, and if you're not going to university you'll have to get a job, and a trade is a better option than unskilled labour," my father declared.

My dad was a builder and my older brother was already doing a carpentry apprenticeship with him, and the two of them were busy driving each other mad. My father had no intention of making that mistake twice.

"We don't need another carpenter in the family," he stated flatly. "That leaves plumbing—digging up poo pipes but decent money, electrician—again okay money, but lots of crawling in roof spaces and under houses, or bricklaying. Bricklayers earn good money and they knock off early."

"Bricklaying sounds good to me," I shrugged.

"Good," Dad remarked. "It'll also help you lose some weight."

Cheers, Dad.

The next day he rang three bricklayers he knew. The first two turned him down but the third one was German like my father, and they both had the same name: Werner. Werner gave me a chance and I started the following Monday.

I often wonder how many others career start out like mine, the result of a happy accident or a lazy kid and a disgruntled dad. I'm a firm believer that the cream always rises to the top and that hard

The Happy Bricklayer
Mark Bayer

work and determination can bring success to anyone. Still, it's a hell of a lot easier if you like your job.

So off I went and began my career on a building site. The main things I had going for me were that I was a hard worker and a good saver. And with that mentality, I spent most of the next twenty years sacrificing more and more time to accumulate more money. Right after my apprenticeship, at the age of 21, I decided to start working for myself. Of course, that choice was all about money. I knew I could make more money in my own business, but I could also work more hours. Which meant even *more* money.

At this stage I was saving for my first home. I didn't live extravagantly, and the hard work was going towards my future. And what was that future dream I was working towards? It was to be NOT WORKING. Looking back, the warning signs were there already. A 21 year-old wanting to *retire*? If you're doing what you love, retirement never even enters your thoughts.

A couple of years later, I met the love of my life, Belinda. We got married when I was 24 and we bought our first home straight after our wedding. It was just a tiny two-bedroom home with an outside toilet—chilly in the winter when you needed to go! But I still remember that amazing feeling when I bought my first property. *It's mine!* I gloated. *Well, mostly it's the bank's, but some of it's mine.*

The Happy Bricklayer
Mark Bayer

Over the next three years we poured all our time and money into extending our house into a five-bedroom, three-bathroom, two-storey extravaganza. It was a lovely home when we were finished, but I was showing the first signs of exhaustion. Not to mention, I was starting to get really bitter about my job—and I was just 27 years old.

Each day I woke up in the dark to a 5 AM alarm, made it to the site by 6:30, laid bricks, and supervised my team of bricklayers until after 4 PM. On top of that I was spending hours in traffic to and from work, plus I also worked most Saturdays. The few spare hours I had left were spent on the house. Of course, my health began to suffer. I had carpal tunnel injuries in my wrists and back problems from the heavy lifting, not to mention dietary issues from eating bad food on the run.

Yearning for change, I convinced my wife that a working holiday in the UK would be a great experience. My brother had been living there for years and loved it, and thanks to our British mother we had a right of abode in England. No visas needed at all! Just weeks after finishing work on our house, we rented it out and headed to the UK.

For the next four years we lived in London and travelled all around the UK and Europe, as well as trips to the US, Canada, and Africa. Once you get bitten by the travel bug, it's hard to stop! London is still my favourite city in the world. Sydney's a great place

The Happy Bricklayer
Mark Bayer

to live with the beaches and the weather, but I've missed London every day since we left.

I never stopped working, though—there was plenty of bricklaying work in Europe! I managed to cope with the repetitive work by keeping myself distracted. London was full of pubs, football, partying, pubs and the amazing city of London, and did I mention the pubs? After more than three years in London Belinda fell pregnant, and we decided it was time to come home to Australia.

Returning to the home we had built and starting a young family surrounded by family and friends was fantastic, but I was determined to get off the trowel and try a new career path. A friend who was a foreman at a civil company offered me a post, and I was hoping for a job like his, off the tools. But they didn't have a foreman position available, and after three months of labouring on low money, I knew I could make a better living in bricklaying. The lure of money combined with the responsibility of supporting a family were too much to resist. I did what was best for them and started building brick walls again.

The Happy Bricklayer
Mark Bayer

> ## Deep thoughts for you to ponder:
>
> - How many teenagers (let alone adults!) know what career they want?
> - Parents mean well, but their advice can be limited.
> - It's your job that you don't like, not the alarm clock.
> - You're never too old to make a change.

OK, now I've told you my sad tale of being stuck in a job I didn't like.

Now I want YOU to think about some of those elements in YOUR life.

The Happy Bricklayer
Mark Bayer

BRICK ONE: Taking Stock of Where You Are Now

How did you end up in your current job?

Did you know what you wanted to do when you were in high school?

The Happy Bricklayer
Mark Bayer

Do you want to change your job?

What is your ideal job, your dream job?

The Happy Bricklayer
Mark Bayer

What's stopping you from making the change?
Is your dream job bricklaying but you are an author? This book is for YOU!

2. Your Life Is A Manifestation of The Thoughts in Your Head

All through my thirties I dreaded going to work every day, but at least I had a life at home with my family. Coming home, building forts out of cushions and having tea parties and wrestling on the rug, I was able to switch off from my career woes by spending time with Belinda and the kids. Apart from those few precious family hours, I was depressed about my position and feeling trapped. I complained about it to anyone who would listen. And oddly, it was at about this time I took my first step towards being happy—though it would take a decade before I finally got there.

One night I went to my mother's house for dinner, and she handed me a DVD, insisting I'd get a lot out of it. "Oprah says you can change your life with this, but I'd be happy if you just stopped moaning all the time!"

Bit harsh coming from a whingeing pom, I thought.

It was a documentary called *The Secret,* and I'd never heard of it. But that movie had a huge impact on me—as it has on millions of other people.

The Happy Bricklayer
Mark Bayer

For those of you who haven't seen the movie or read the book, the main theme is something called the "law of attraction." Now, I'm no philosopher. I'm a bricklayer. And here's a bricklayer's description of the law of attraction:

By constantly imagining what we want, our subconscious mind will steer us toward our goals. If we visualise ourselves living our ideal life, we will attract that life to us. At the subconscious level, our minds don't distinguish between what we see and what we imagine, so if we keep imagining ourselves living our ideal life, our subconscious mind will plot a course to get us there. Unfortunately, most of us go around focusing on the negative things in our current lives, so we end up attracting more of the same.

For me, watching *The Secret* was like a slap in the face, *wham!* For years I'd been waking up every day to the grinding buzz of a horrible alarm clock, starting my day focusing on everything I hated about my job. I used all my mental energy to focus on the negatives: how much I hated driving in city traffic, dealing with unreliable staff, getting sunburnt in the summer, freezing in the winter, plus dealing with rain and wind. Not to mention the mind-numbingly boring task of 50 HOURS A WEEK of repetitive bricklaying, one after the other, and another, and another, mud, bricks, mud, bricks, repeat, rewind, and do it again.

The Happy Bricklayer
Mark Bayer

But when I saw *The Secret*, I began to look at things in a whole new light...

Do you know what I realised at that moment? Bricklaying was *nowhere near as bad* as I was making it out to be. I had been acknowledging only the negative parts of my job and replaying those thoughts in my mind, over and over. In fact, I started to recognise all the positive things my bricklaying work had given me. I had a huge new home in a great area when most of my mates were still renting. I was able to work overseas and travel with my trade. I'd built my own home with the skills I'd learned on building sites, and helped my family and friends work on their homes with those same skills. And every single day, I got to see huge progress on the home construction projects of all my happy customers.

For the first time, I realized the power in our own minds. If I learned to control my mind like a Jedi, I could use my imagination for good instead of evil. My brain was now seeing a green lightsabre instead of a red one. *Fuck you Darth Vader, I'm taking back control!*

The next day at work, I was happier than I'd been in a decade. I was so thankful for everything my trade had helped me achieve. I felt respect for bricklaying now. Of course, it wasn't *that* easy: I didn't get brainwashed overnight into loving my day-to-day life. I still craved a change, but now I was focused on the future instead of the past. I had taken my first step to living a life of fulfilment.

The Happy Bricklayer
Mark Bayer

It's a funny thing about bricklaying. You could have two bricklayers working side by side: one thinks he's building a prison and the other thinks he's building a magnificent cathedral. Only one of them feels elevated and ennobled by his work—but they're both laying the same old bricks! Like the saying about a glass half-full or a glass half-empty, it's your choice how you view things. You CAN choose to ignore the negatives and focus purely on the positives—I did.

The Happy Bricklayer
Mark Bayer

Deep thoughts for you to ponder:

- We are what we think! If you focus on the negative aspects of your work, you will invite discontent.
- You have complete control over how you view your job and your life.
- Focusing on the positives of your job will make it more pleasant to be there as you work towards a positive change.
- Oprah knows her shit! Just ask my mum.

Ready to take on the dark side?

Put down your red lightsabre, and pick up the green one!

The Happy Bricklayer
Mark Bayer

BRICK TWO: Re-Imagining Your Current Job

Make a list of all the positives about your current job.

List as many as you can think of! Every job has some positives—you probably just haven't thought much about them lately.

Now you see the positives, focus on being thankful for your job. You don't have to be content to do it forever, it's easier to plan a change for the better when you focus on the positives.

The Happy Bricklayer
Mark Bayer

What skills from your current job are you proud of?

Do you have any colleagues you enjoy working with?

The Happy Bricklayer
Mark Bayer

Could you work toward a role where you do more of the positive parts of your job?

What are you passionate about?

The Happy Bricklayer
Mark Bayer

What will your average day look like when you are living your ideal life?

Who is that one total dick at your current job you will be glad to see the ass end of?

3. The Law of Attraction

Now it was time to start focusing on my ideal life, but what was that? I knew what I didn't want, and that was to spend another 20 years bricklaying. But I was stuck. *What do I love? What am I passionate about?* I was willing to take a minimum wage job if I loved the work, but I had no idea where to start. Finally, I started Googling.

I typed in *jobs for happiness* and started to search. One of the first things I found was an ad for someone to help me achieve happiness, something called a "life coach." *Pfft!* I snorted. *I'm after a new career, not some incense-burning hippy to listen to my problems!* But for some reason, I read on. It turns out, a life coach is someone who helps identify a client's goals and uses tools based on psychology to help them achieve those goal in a specified period of time.

That intrigued me. I thought, *What a great job, helping people like me achieve their dreams!* I started to research all about life coaching—and straightaway I found myself enthralled by the idea of doing it for a job. The courses were mostly distance education, with only a few days of face-to-face learning. I could do the diploma in my spare time. In a blaze of enthusiasm, I rang several

The Happy Bricklayer
Mark Bayer

businesses and learned which of the training providers I preferred, which course they were offering, and where they were located. Then I found out the catch: training to be a life coach cost $6,600.00.

I talked it over with Belinda. She was a stay-at-home mum at the time, caring for our young daughter Bella. Money was tight. She didn't say no, but she did express some hesitation. "It's a lot of money—are you sure?" she asked. And that question amplified the little voice of responsibility inside my head. *I can't be so selfish*, I thought. *It's a lot of money.*

So I put my plans on hold. I did what I always did and kept on bricklaying, but the seed was planted. I couldn't stop thinking about becoming a life coach. I chatted to everyone about it at work, explaining what a life coach was and what they did. I got a fair few funny looks, as not many fellas on a building site had ever heard about "life coaching," but it still absorbed my every thought.

A few weeks later I had an appointment with a new accountant, as my old one had moved overseas. I took all my papers and handed them over. Filomena had a very successful practice and she asked me all about my family as we discussed my taxes. I told her about our travels, our new baby, and Belinda making the choice to stay home with our daughter.

The Happy Bricklayer
Mark Bayer

"Well, I have some good news for you," Filomena smiled. "Your old accountant did your 2004 return but never claimed your refund." It was now 2009.

"So I'm owed money?" I wanted to know. "How much?"

(Any guesses, anyone?)

Filomena pushed the return toward me and pointed. "$6,600."

"Get fucked," I replied.

After apologizing for my language, I explained to Filomena how absolutely crazy it was that my tax refund was in that specific amount. Filomena demanded I enrol in the life coaching course immediately—it was just too much of a coincidence. I rushed home, told Belinda, and she agreed.

I enrolled that night.

Deep thoughts for you to ponder:

- Don't ignore a coincidence!
- Be on the lookout for a signal of any kind telling you to make a change.

Have you searched online for a job with happy endings? Massage therapist might be an option!

The Happy Bricklayer
Mark Bayer

BRICK THREE: Setting Your Sights On A New Path

Do you know of anyone who works in the field you are interested in? Can you ask for their advice?

Not all jobs require qualifications! What are some skills you can learn from free resources like the library to help you towards a career change?

The Happy Bricklayer
Mark Bayer

Is it possible to get work experience in your chosen field? Many people have gained employment after impressing employers during work experience.

Is your dream job bricklaying and you're looking for some work experience? Feel free to get in touch with me.

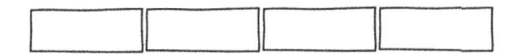

4. Life Coaching

Once I booked my life coaching course, work became more tolerable. I felt invigorated and I had a new focus, knowing that I was on my way to building a more satisfying career and life. I spent my days on the building site dreaming about my new career, and I never focused on the negative parts of bricklaying. I envisioned myself in my coaching practise chatting with clients, working from home, and not having to travel in my new career. Altogether, the future looked awesome!

The life coaching course began with a three-day class on the Gold Coast, so Belinda and our baby daughter Bella flew up with me for a short getaway. It was a fantastic experience. For three days, I got to meet a group of people from all walks of life, each of whom shared the same goal: to create satisfying careers that helped people.

We learned some amazing tools during those three days that I've used ever since, like Neuro-Linguistic Programming. Look, I'm no neurologist, but I'll give you the bricklayer's interpretation of Neuro-Linguistic Programming. Basically, it's the way we communicate with

The Happy Bricklayer
Mark Bayer

others using both language and actions, to help get their behaviour aligned with their goals.

Sounds fancy, right? It's not.

I learned about something called *mirroring*, where you mirror people's body language to build rapport faster, like copying the way they stand or talk. I learned the art of *listening*: as it turns out, a good coach does very little talking; he/she asks transformative questions that evoke amazing responses.

Learning all this new information transformed my view on life. I started practicing life coaching on fellow students over the phone, and they started coaching me back. During this time, I came up with several new goals to improve my life, and I planned to work towards them successfully.

One day, I was having a session with a fellow student when I uncovered some interesting things. "If you won the lottery," he asked me, "what would you do with your time?"

That floored me.

What WOULD I do?

Because I *did* have a passion, one I'd been ignoring for a long time: writing.

I knew all at once that if I won the lottery I would finally finish writing the stories I'd started, the ones I've got stuffed in the back of a drawer. But writing always seemed self-indulgent, and I only ever

The Happy Bricklayer
Mark Bayer

did it on holiday. I thought maybe I'd devote my energy to it later in life, when I was retired and had the time. Of course, if I struck it rich I'd travel the world and do exotic things, but alongside that, I couldn't ignore the stories. I wanted to finish them. I wanted to *write*.

Then my fellow student asked me another question. *If you were to die, would you have any regrets?*

Again, I thought about the writing. I started those stories so long ago. If I were to die without giving myself the time to complete them, I knew it would be a massive regret. Of course, I'd miss watching my children grow up and start families of their own, but if I died tomorrow, I knew my greatest personal regret would always be those unwritten stories.

Writing was something I first experimented with back in high school, when I was selected for a creative writing class. I really enjoyed it at the time, but after that it stopped being a priority. Later, as a young adult, I found myself constantly brainstorming ideas for movies. I'd discuss them with friends, colleagues, and family—and I'd scribble all my ideas down in books. I must have 100 notebooks scattered around the house, with different scene ideas that have fluttered through my thoughts. And there's hundreds more stored on my phone.

The Happy Bricklayer
Mark Bayer

Now *this* was interesting. I was training to be a life coach, but when I looked inside, *writing* was what my heart yearned for. But I didn't yet realize how important that was. For the moment, I ignored all the signals.

One of the final tasks in my life coaching course was to do some free sessions with volunteers. I'd enjoyed the sessions with my classmates, and I was starting to develop my own coaching style. Now I just needed volunteers. Easy, huh?

Well, I spent weeks calling and emailing all of my friends. I couldn't get ANYONE. It was so disheartening. As soon as I asked if I could do some life coaching, the barriers went up. Mostly the reasons were "I don't need counselling," or "there's nothing wrong with me!" I'd try to explain what life coaching was—it wasn't counselling! It was finding an area of your life that needs improvement and then forming a strategy to achieve your goals! It was a *good thing!*

"Yeah no thanks," one friend told me, "Do I look like I'm a few sandwiches short a picnic or something?"

"No," I told him. "But you do have a face like a bucket of burnt Lego. Maybe try plastic surgery if coaching isn't your thing!"

Looking back, I was so disillusioned. I couldn't even find a volunteer to give my services for free! How the hell was I going to get someone to *pay* me to do it? It didn't help that during one of our

The Happy Bricklayer
Mark Bayer

last video calls with a teacher, he mentioned that fewer than 5% of students end up as full-time life coaches. *Wish he'd mentioned that before I handed over my tax windfall.*

It wasn't a conscious decision, but I slowly stopped talking about being a life coach with family and friends. Instead, I went back to bricklaying—and life went on. But that training session wasn't a waste of time, far from it. I still use what I learned in that course all the time when I'm advising my friends. And it's funny—no one wanted my free life coaching sessions, but I'm often the person they call for advice, or just to offload. And the real surprise? Turns out, learning about life coaching was the first time I realised how important writing really is to me.

The Happy Bricklayer
Mark Bayer

> Deep thoughts for you to ponder:
>
> - Knowing you want a change is easy.
> - Discovering what you want to change to ISN'T easy.
> - Change for the sake of change may bring temporary relief, but to find what will make you truly happy, you might need to seek out help.

Have you experience in fraud, deception and hypocrisy? You could easily transfer those skills and become a politician!

The Happy Bricklayer
Mark Bayer

BRICK FOUR: Who Are You, Anyway?

What were your favourite classes in school?
What subjects were you best in at school?

The Happy Bricklayer
Mark Bayer

What are you passionate about?

What does the world need?

The Happy Bricklayer
Mark Bayer

What are your hobbies outside of work?

What are you proud of?

The Happy Bricklayer
Mark Bayer

What work has given you the most satisfaction so far?

What work have you received praise for in the past?

The Happy Bricklayer
Mark Bayer

What are your natural talents?

How much money do you need to make you happy?

The Happy Bricklayer
Mark Bayer

What could you compromise on?

Would you like to be your own boss?

The Happy Bricklayer
Mark Bayer

Are you willing to move for work?

Do you prefer working in a team or on your own?

The Happy Bricklayer
Mark Bayer

> Do You know any good wife coaches? Please forward their details to the happy bricklayer.

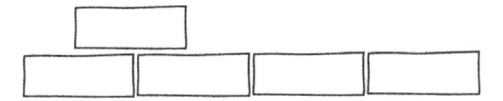

5. Fear of Failure

Fear of failure was a common theme in my life, and now I felt like I'd failed again. Here I'd spent all that money on life coaching training, only to give it up later. Why did I waste the money and time on a course, then never even start trying to grow a practice?

I found myself envying people who seemed content with their jobs. Take my wife Belinda, for example. She has two degrees, works as a radiographer, and she loves it. She enjoys helping others and finds the work is interesting. I'm sure she'd like more money and more holidays, but in general she's content to continue her profession until she retires.

Me, on the other hand? I started looking for the next quick buck.

A few years after the life coaching course, our son Ewan was born and we decided to move closer to the beach and build a new home. I built it myself while working full-time in bricklaying, once again stretching myself to my physical limit.

The demands of a newborn and building a new house distracted me from my despair for a while, but as soon as the house

The Happy Bricklayer
Mark Bayer

was done I was back in my cycle of whingeing discontent. I started casting around for possible business ventures.

My business partner and I had saved a little money and we bought an investment property outside of Sydney. We renovated the existing house and built a second house on the land, then rented them both out. That kept me busy for a while. But once that project was completed, I started looking for new ways to make money.

And that's when I came up with an idea for an app. I called it "Amplify Live," an app that allowed you to pay for song requests and dedications at live music gigs, with pub cover bands and DJs. I figured Amplify Live would give the audience control of the music and earn the artists some extra cash. Plus, the piss-take possibilities were endless: imagine embarrassing your mates at the pub by dedicating a love song from one to the other, or making a fake announcement about their engagement.

Now. When it comes to computers, there's one thing you should know: I'm about as useless as tits on a bull. Not that I let that fact dissuade me. *Apps are easy money!* I thought. *We'll all be rich!* I predicted.

Well, how wrong I was.

We started looking into what was involved in building an app. We hired a consulting business to workshop our idea, and we had a detailed business plan in place, with fancy fonts and everything.

The Happy Bricklayer
Mark Bayer

Friends and family members thought my idea was great, and that was encouraging, but it also just fed my creative ego. The cost of building an app was *huge*—way more than we ever imagined. Nonetheless, we borrowed money against our investment property and persevered. The app took over six months to build, and over time the budget ballooned.

It wasn't until our product was finished that we came to realize we were in over our heads. It's all well and good to build the thing—how do you market an app? How do you get people to use it? What about updates and bug fixes to keep it working? We'd budgeted just enough to build the damned thing, then hopefully it would start paying us back. The reality was, it was costing us thousands a month to keep it functional, and that's without spending a cent on marketing.

Since then, I've discovered that for every great app idea like Uber or Instagram, there are tens of thousands like ours that never make it. My heart still says we had a good idea. But we simply didn't have any more money to burn, so we stopped altogether. All in all, my get-rich-quick scheme cost us over $200,000. *Yikes.*

I know I was fortunate to have that money to risk on a business venture, and not everyone does. But starting a business doesn't have to cost $200K, far from it. In fact, I could have tried to get investors on board from the beginning. That can be a great way

The Happy Bricklayer
Mark Bayer

of testing your ideas—if no one's willing to invest, then perhaps you need to spend more time on the business plan. If we had been more thorough we would have been aware of marketing costs before starting.

It was an expensive lesson, but I did learn one thing: avoid businesses you have no experience in. Funny thing is, I don't regret it at all. Sure, I wish I had the money back—but it felt good to try something new and create an invention from my own mind. *Aha! Another clue...being creative brings me joy.*

If you read many books written by successful people, you'll find they all failed multiple times before they found success. Many successful entrepreneurs have been bankrupt in their past. It's the ability to dust yourself off after failure, believe in yourself, and give it another go that makes the difference. And that's exactly what I've done.

There was another lesson here I needed to remember as well. Our app idea was great. It could still be successful. But it never got off the ground because of my lack of planning. I was trying to build without a solid foundation—and as a bricklayer, I should have known better! Looking back, I realize how silly I was to jump into something new without having every step carefully planned out.

Yes, we planned; yes, we researched. But we didn't do anywhere near as much as we should have. If we had, we would have

The Happy Bricklayer
Mark Bayer

learned that we needed a massive amount of marketing money. We would have found out that we needed ongoing staff to maintain the app, update it, and improve it.

I'm a bricklayer. Why in the world did I think I could strike it rich with an app? Well, I'm sure if I had a great coach at the time quizzing me, we would have dug down to the heart of the matter: my drive to create the app was about making a passive income. I just wanted to free up some time, so I could work on writing my stories.

Years later, I now have a brick-by-brick plan of how to achieve my dreams. The detail is immense and it took time to write, because I didn't know how to take some of my steps. I know YOU can put together the same thing. Sometimes you'll have to ask for help and have others explain things to you, but it's 100% possible to work it out.

I'll tell you one thing: you can never have too much detail or too many steps. A wall can have thousands of bricks in it—the greater the quantity, the greater the wall. It may seem huge, but with the right planning I promise it's possible.

Take this book, for example. Each chapter is a brick in my wall. Finishing this book was a milestone on my journey to becoming a successful author.

Spending time planning out your brick-by-brick plan is critical to assuring you'll get to your goal. A detailed plan is your strong

The Happy Bricklayer
Mark Bayer

foundation. If you skimp on the details, you're just setting yourself up for failure.

Just ask the Three Little Pigs—you know, those little porkers from the children's story. If you rush the planning part, your whole house could tumble down around you like it did for those first two lazy little pigs. It might take you weeks or months to detail every step of your journey. You can't knock it out in a few hours. You have to identify every single necessary step, then break each step into small, achievable tasks that you can complete each day. And just like the third little pig, you lay each task brick-by-brick, giving you a mighty foundation that will ensure you complete your goal (and keep out that nasty wolf.)

No short cuts!

Failure is an opportunity to learn

The Happy Bricklayer
Mark Bayer

Deep thoughts for you to ponder:

- All successful people have failed before. They refused to give up!
- Make sure your career change will satisfy your sense of purpose.
- A detailed plan is necessary! It will be your strong foundation to build your new life from.

Don't waste your time with a house made of straw.
Take your time, plan your foundation, and build a house out of bricks!

The Happy Bricklayer
Mark Bayer

BRICK FIVE: A Brick-By-Brick Plan to Build A Better Life

What's not working in your life right now?

What are your most important values?

The Happy Bricklayer
Mark Bayer

What do you want to achieve?

What do you want to change?

The Happy Bricklayer
Mark Bayer

What would you like to accomplish?

What obstacles are there to overcome?

The Happy Bricklayer
Mark Bayer

What activities make you feel alive and give you a sense of fulfilment?

If money were no object, how would you spend your time?

The Happy Bricklayer
Mark Bayer

What are your core values?

What steps have you taken to achieve your goals?

The Happy Bricklayer
Mark Bayer

How motivated are you to achieve your goals?

What are your biggest fears?

The Happy Bricklayer
Mark Bayer

What are your specific goals?

What would it mean to you to achieve those goals?

On a scale of 1 to 10, how committed are you to achieving your goals?

Are you ready to do whatever it takes to achieve your goals?

The Happy Bricklayer
Mark Bayer

What steps are necessary for you to take to achieve your goals?

How confident are you in your ability to achieve success?

The Happy Bricklayer
Mark Bayer

What can you do to improve your confidence in reaching your goal?

Describe what your life will look like when you are living your dream life?

The Happy Bricklayer
Mark Bayer

How will you know when you have achieved success?

Do you refer to a poker machine as a bricklayer's laptop?

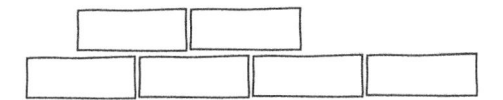

6. Making A Change

About six years ago, my business partner Rado was growing tired of life as a bricklayer, just like me. He enjoyed carpentry and he spent his spare time pulling apart machines and tinkering with things. And he was already well on his way to a change. With a lot of hard work and study, he'd finally earned his builders license.

So now he was trying to convince me to quit the bricks and start doing building work. Eventually, he wore me down. We made the decision to leave bricklaying behind and start a building company, focused on renovations.

Part of the reason we made the change was that building meant working with subcontractors, which was easier than the responsibility of having permanent employees. This way we could take more time off, and that worked fine for me. My children were both in school now, and I didn't want to work Saturdays or school holidays.

After more than two decades as a bricklayer, becoming a builder was a huge about turn. I still had early starts, and I still worked on construction sites, but I was freed from the tedium of laying those never-ending bricks. We did a variety of work:

The Happy Bricklayer
Mark Bayer

excavation, steel work, concreting, carpentry, roofing, Gyprocking, and painting, and project management of course.

The only change I didn't like was my new lack of confidence. In brickwork, I'd been at the top of my trade. I could do anything—I had an excellent professional reputation and I was in high demand. As a builder, I...wasn't. Most builders start out as carpenters, then they complete a builder's course, and I had done neither. Rado had the license and the knowledge, and I learned a lot from him. But many times, when I was talking with clients, I felt incompetent and as useful as a glass hammer.

The main role of a builder is project management, and at least that was *one* thing I was good at. But when it comes to carpentry, I wasn't the sharpest chisel in the pouch. It was hard to make sure my tradesmen were working correctly when I didn't have the faintest idea what their work was supposed to look like.

My skills improved a bit as the years went by. I was now putting my underwear under my tool belt, not over it, but I was still coming to work with anxiety. I was constantly worried I'd make a mistake or worse yet, someone would find out I was a total fraud. Rado told me to go learn some carpentry, but I didn't listen. The truth is, I just didn't have any interest in building. I was coming to work for the money, not for any love of the trade.

The Happy Bricklayer
Mark Bayer

Sure, I'd had the courage to change my career, but this wasn't my dream job. I had a little more stimulation and variety in my day, but I definitely wasn't excited about going to work. That feeling of discontent lingered on, because I had no sense of purpose.

Even after all the books I'd read, even with all the courses I'd done, I still couldn't take the leap and build a life of true happiness—one that was better than "just okay."

I was given a book by a friend once. In it, the author observed that from a young age, we all get graded at school. When we're bad at a particular subject, we're told to spend more time on that class to improve our grades. And according to this guy, that's just backwards. In actual fact, we *shouldn't* be focusing on subjects we're no good at, because in all likelihood we have no interest in them. Instead, we should put more emphasis on the subjects we ARE good at, because those are the ones we're more likely to enjoy, and that's where we'll have the best chance at success.

It makes sense, doesn't it? When I think back to the subjects I was good at in high school, like creative writing, I enjoyed the lessons and I put in the effort without any encouragement. I did the assignments, I wrote the stories, I looked forward to each class and I thoroughly enjoyed the creative process. But in the classes where I struggled, every day was a nightmare—and I dragged my feet getting *anything* done.

The Happy Bricklayer
Mark Bayer

When it came time to choose the classes for my final years of high school, they told us to pick subjects that would help us toward our chosen profession. "Yeah na," I rolled my eyes. "No idea what I want to do as a career, so that's a no." Then I got this idea into my head that if I chose the hardest possible subjects, the marking system would scale up my scores, giving me higher grades. That was the worst decision of my schooling career. Looking back, if I'd just picked subjects I enjoyed and was good at, I probably wouldn't have dropped out of school.

Even today, there's a kind of stigma attached to creative classes, and even more so for boys. Lots of people think subjects like art, music, cooking, writing, fashion, drama, and photography are nothing more than a waste of time. They assume you can't get into university or find a good job with those classes, but that's just not true. These days it's popular to push kids into maths and the sciences so they can track into highly-paid professions, but that seems like a mistake to me. Focusing on what we're good at is the best place to start looking at careers. It's better to be a happy bricklayer than a sad, rich lawyer!

I had a friend called Rob who I used to do some weight training with in my 20's, and Rob was looking to make some money from a side hustle, as his day job was in construction. His wife had bought a modelling agency and would occasionally have a few jobs

The Happy Bricklayer
Mark Bayer

come up, suitable for Rob. He was a good-looking guy, tall and muscular, Maltese heritage so olive skin and dark hair. His wife had him turn up to a photo shoot for an advertisement in a park in the CBD. He was nervous as he had never done any modelling before, especially with his shirt off. He was required to stand in just his underwear in a Vitruvian man type pose with a large yoga ball above his head. There were other people in the photo shoot, a bit of a circus type group, with Rob being the strong man type character. The shoot was taking a while and Rob was allowed to rest a while between shoots and he decided to sit on top of the gym ball that he was holding, one that had been borrowed from a nearby gym. Well as he sat down on the gym ball, Rob had failed to notice someone throw a still burning cigarette butt on the ground and he sat the ball right on top of it, and of course as he sat all his weight on the ball it exploded with a loud bang and everyone turned towards him to see him fall comically backwards, legs in the air and land on his back.

Needless to say, Rob never modelled again, he was mortified as they were unable to find another ball and had to make do with the shots they already had. Rob had attempted a new change and swiftly decided it wasn't for him. It obviously wasn't satisfying his sense of purpose.

There was a boy when I was in high school who bucked the trend and chose cooking when all the other boys chose sport, and I

The Happy Bricklayer
Mark Bayer

remember someone questioned his sexuality. His reply was epic. "Yeah, I'm eating brownies with 30 girls whilst you're showering with 30 sweaty boys, and you're calling ME gay?!" It was a great response, but I don't know if cooking really was his sense of purpose!

If you are interested in looking into your personality type and suitable careers, Google Clifton StrengthsFinder. You can pay to take a questionnaire that evaluates your strengths, and you might be surprised with your results! Everyone can benefit from evaluating their strengths and weaknesses, and it's even better if kids are encouraged to do it in high school. That way, they'll be more likely to pick a career that's more aligned with their strengths. Sure, that means we'll need to create a lot more jobs for gamers, influencers and Tik Tok dancers—but so be it!

The Happy Bricklayer
Mark Bayer

Deep thoughts for you to ponder:

- Your new job should involve skills that come naturally to you and that you enjoy!
- If the study or training is boring you, then that job is not the one for you.
- Whilst we all need money to live, doing a job you love will make you FEEL rich.

Stop trying to improve your weaknesses. Instead, make time for what you're best at!

The Happy Bricklayer
Mark Bayer

BRICK SIX: Examining Your Strengths

What are your character strengths?

What are you good at?

The Happy Bricklayer
Mark Bayer

What do you enjoy doing?

What jobs have these qualities?

The Happy Bricklayer
Mark Bayer

Have you explored all industries ?

Do you refer to a butt crack as bricklayer's cleavage?

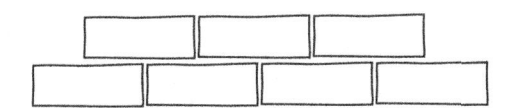

7. The Grass Isn't Always Greener

After 12 years in business together, Rado and I decided to separate the company. It wasn't lost on Rado that I'd been going through the motions these past few years, and he decided he needed a new direction. Before he left the business, he helped me get my builders license so I could continue building without him—but that sense of incompetence I had? It just got worse without him there to lean on.

After a while, I started hunting around on a job website. After all, if Rado could make a change, what was stopping me to from trying something new? When I looked back over my 25-year career, I decided my favourite part of the job was quoting. I enjoy measuring up and working out the costs, but mostly I love meeting the clients and selling myself as the potential builder and bricklayer. I began looking at jobs in home sales, always face-to-face, not over the phone or in a premise. I'd been interested in the solar boom that was happening around roof panels and batteries. The whole industry was screaming out for more salesman, and they were offering good money, too. But time and again, I'd look at a job, think to myself *sounds perfect,* and just...never apply.

The Happy Bricklayer
Mark Bayer

Somewhere deep down, I knew: if I were to get that sales job, I wouldn't be living my dream life. If I got a sales job, I'd make a good living. But it would be taking up time and attention, holding me back from my dream of being a writer. Selling is just not my sense of purpose.

This was a HUGE moment in my life. I had finally realised what my sense of purpose was. A new career in sales could be a better option than bricklaying, but if it wasn't my absolute passion, after awhile I would find myself in exactly the same rut. You see, each time I made a change I was just focused on escaping bricklaying. The many money-making schemes I had tried were always aimed at securing a passive income. I didn't aspire to become a billionaire or a big CEO. I just wanted enough money to retire, so I could spend time writing my stories.

And that's when I realised: I didn't want to retire. I wanted to become a writer.

On some level I'd always known that, but I'd never entertained the idea that I could be a successful enough writer to make a living from it. Sure, I fantasized about selling movie scripts to Hollywood or having a best-selling book published, but deep down I thought it wasn't possible. For now, just the thought of actually completing those stories I'd started was a big enough dream for me.

The Happy Bricklayer
Mark Bayer

And I didn't come up with that realization all on my own. I had help from a hypnotherapist I met along the way, when I was trying to lose weight. Eventually, Lauren and I got to talking about my writing. I told her it was just a hobby, but Lauren challenged me on that.

"Why *can't* you become a successful writer?" she asked. "What's stopping you? A fear of failure?"

"Well, I have to work to provide for my family," I insisted.

But Lauren persevered. "Wouldn't your family be happier to see you follow your dreams and be doing what you love every day?"

THAT was a wake-up call.

And that's when I started making real changes in my life.

I decided that I wasn't yet willing to quit my job completely. I still felt the need to provide for my family, but thanks to my decades of hard work bricklaying, I had set us up financially. I didn't really need to work full-time. My wife Belinda was working, and we had some passive income off investment properties. That was enough. So I came up with the idea of working part-time in construction, and part- time writing. It was the perfect compromise.

Ever since then, I've implemented a hybrid building-writing schedule. It fluctuates, and I allow for that. I like to write a few days a week, but sometimes bigger building projects make that difficult, so I make up for it by taking a few weeks off between those larger

The Happy Bricklayer
Mark Bayer

projects. I started exercising again, too, and I'm the lightest I've been in 15 years. I've even entered a half-marathon race later this year!

Deep thoughts for you to ponder:

- Why NOT a creative job? There's no reason why YOU can't be a successful artist, writer, or musician.
- The right coach or therapist can help unlock the things that have been holding you back.
- Make sure the change you make is ticking ALL your boxes, not just getting you away from your current job.

Time to stop making excuses.
What's stopping YOU from starting your dream life?

The Happy Bricklayer
Mark Bayer

BRICK SEVEN: Setting Aside the Distractions

Have you taken jobs for their high pay, even when you knew you wouldn't enjoy them?
What is stopping you from making the changes in your life to lead a satisfying and content existence?

The Happy Bricklayer
Mark Bayer

> Will donating 10% of your income to "The Happy Bricklayer Cult" improve your happiness?

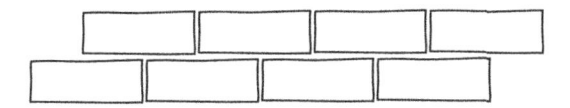

8. A Sense of Purpose

For years, hundreds of movie scenes flooded my imagination, and I just ignored them. Instead of recognising that I wanted to be a writer, when I got bored with my career I started casting about for a new job to pay the bills. But of course, that's a huge mistake: finding your sense of purpose is integral to finding happiness. I wasn't ready to accept that writing was my purpose. I just knew I couldn't be a bricklayer anymore.

It wasn't till I was in my 40's that I finally committed to becoming a writer. I had been ignoring all the signs that had been flooding my brain for decades. Having Lauren expose the mental barriers that were holding me back from considering writing as an actual career felt like a miracle to me. Finding our sense of purpose is rarely something people discover in their childhood. You need to experience life a little and try different things before you start to find your passions.

Too often, we end up getting stuck in the first option we try. We start earning a living, we become dependent on our income, and we get used to the living standards that income provides. The thought of starting all over again just feels too hard, so we give up

The Happy Bricklayer
Mark Bayer

on our dreams and find small moments of pleasure to satisfy us, like holidays and time with our loved ones.

So, if you can discover that sense of purpose that you feel you were put on this Earth for, and have the belief that there is a way that you can make a living out of doing it, then you are on your way to build you dream life. You have already laid your first bricks.

Now that I'm able to spend several full days a week writing, I'm feeling that sense of purpose that I yearned for all along. I still work part-time as a bricklayer, and I'll keep doing that until I start making money from my writing. But it's a lot easier going to work on a building site when I know that in a few days I'll be back at the keyboard, working towards my goal! In fact, these days my time on the trowel allows my mind to wander, and I can spend my time brainstorming ideas. (And that's another reminder that there are some positives to my bricklaying trade!)

If you know what your sense of purpose is, but it isn't a job you can monetize, it can be difficult to commit. For example, you may yearn to be an artist but you think it's too hard to make money, so you'll do it as a hobby instead. And that's okay. But why *can't* you be an artist earning a living off your work? It IS possible, you just have to work out a way of making it happen. Some people do—why not you? You can find a way. Talk to successful people in your chosen

The Happy Bricklayer
Mark Bayer

field. Find out how they did it. Research. Study. Formulate a foolproof way of getting there.

When I decided I wanted to be a writer, I joined online writing groups for feedback. I read dozens of books on the writing genres that interest me. I've found professional published writers to edit my work and give me feedback, and their encouragement is fantastic. There are always like-minded people out there to help you achieve your dreams. And you don't always need a professional! If you find another person who is striving for the exact same career, you can help each other with study and feedback—you just have to start looking.

If you're struggling to pinpoint exactly what your sense of purpose is on your own, don't hesitate to use a life coach or a therapist. Remember, you don't have to have "something wrong with you" to see some advice. It amazes me the money people will spend on their hobbies or sports, but they tighten the purse strings when it comes to mental health. Take it from me: having another person's perspective amplifies your results, and you'll feel amazing after your session.

Even if you can only manage to work part-time on your sense of purpose, I'm here to tell you that it feels fantastic. I'm lucky, in that my training is actual the same as my dream. By spending time each week writing my stories, my skills are improving and I'm living

The Happy Bricklayer
Mark Bayer

my dream life, and I will build towards being a published author—one brick at a time.

> # Deep thoughts for you to ponder:
>
> - Your sense of purpose is the reason why you were put on this Earth!
> - Even working part time towards your dream job will make you feel happy and better able to cope at your old job.

Commitment can be a challenge (especially for us blokes), but committing to building your dream life will be the best decision you ever make!

The Happy Bricklayer
Mark Bayer

BRICK EIGHT: Finding Your Sense of Purpose

Have you been ignoring a bombardment of signals from your brain about what you should be doing?

If all jobs were paid equally, what would you choose to do?

The Happy Bricklayer
Mark Bayer

Do you know what your sense of purpose is?
What is it?

The Happy Bricklayer
Mark Bayer

Are there people who make a living from it?

What can you do to make it your job?

The Happy Bricklayer
Mark Bayer

> Is your sense of purpose is to be sitting on the couch, watching sports and eating potato crisps? Then perhaps you can move back into your mum's basement and live the dream.

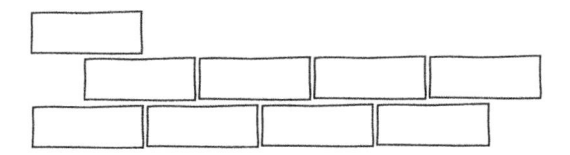

9. Hypnotherapy

I always figured no one could hypnotize me, because I thought you they had to put you to sleep. I couldn't sleep a wink in a long car ride or a flight, so I reckoned there was no way anyone could talk me to sleep and make me cluck like a chicken!

But eventually, a friend convinced me that hypnotherapy would be a great tool to go with my life coaching course. He was a personal trainer and I was open to learning something new. So I put aside my judgment, and I signed up for a two-day training.

I learned some great things that weekend. First of all: yes, I can be hypnotized—but I wasn't actually what you'd call "sleep." You want the bricklayer's version of hypnotherapy? Okay, here we go:

The therapist guides you slowly into a state of tranquillity, and you start by relaxing your mind. Then, the therapist makes suggestions that are absorbed into a deeper level of your subconscious.

I wasn't one of the students that the teacher was able to fully hypnotize, so at least I won that one. I think in a group session he was able to get around four of the 25 participants fully under

The Happy Bricklayer
Mark Bayer

hypnosis, so they would move and act as instructed. But it was an exercise with a classmate that really changed my mind.

We were given scripts to read from, and we took turns hypnotizing one another. We spent a few minutes talking in a relaxed voice, bringing our subject deeper into a trance-like state. I told my classmate I had a helium balloon floating on a string. Then I pretended to tie this imaginary balloon around his wrist, and his arm floated up like it was being pulled by a balloon!

I couldn't believe it. All around the room people were following the same script, and their arms were floating up everywhere. It really worked! I was able to read this simple script and hypnotize someone on my first try.

I was still sceptical, though.

Next it was my turn to be hypnotized. The other student read me the script. *You're feeling calm, going deeper and feeling more and more relaxed*...and when she pretended to tie the string around my wrist, up floated my arm as if the balloon had dragged it into the air. It truly did, without me controlling it.

I was blown away. I wasn't asleep. I *felt* I was totally aware of my surroundings, and yes, I was relaxed, but...*how did that work*? From then on, hypnosis had me intrigued.

The other fascinating thing I learned that weekend was *anchoring*. Want to hear the bricklayer's description? Here it is:

The Happy Bricklayer
Mark Bayer

anchoring is when we associate an internal response or feeling with an external trigger, like a touch. We took turns with this by closing our eyes and relaxing, then we had to find a sad memory, one of the worst memories we'd experienced that we knew would call up feelings of sadness. It was my turn, so I closed my eyes.

For me, what came to mind was the time my childhood dog Pep died. When I was 17, he was 13 and I can't remember him not being part of our family—but back then he was very unwell. He couldn't walk, and he had such severe arthritis that he constantly yelped in pain. We had to clean him all the time as he couldn't even stand or squat to relieve himself. We'd tried so many medications and treatments, and finally the vet convinced us it was time to let him go. My father and sister couldn't watch and they left the room in tears, but I didn't want him to be alone with strangers when they gave him the sedative. I vividly remember his eyes as they slowly closed. He was happy because he was with me, and I'm not sure if he knew what was happening, but he looked like he trusted me and was relieved to be free from the pain.

At that moment, my fellow student squeezed my thumb, exactly when I had that memory in my mind. I guess it could work for any body part, though you probably shouldn't go for somewhere cheeky! That day, we just squeezed our partner's thumb. We

The Happy Bricklayer
Mark Bayer

repeated the exercise with other tragic memories, then we switched places.

We both took a moment to clear our minds, turning our attention to pleasant thoughts. Then the instructor told us to squeeze our thumbs. POW, that same awful feeling returned. Just for a few seconds, I felt the intense grief of losing my best friend in the world—but this time, I wasn't thinking about dogs. I wasn't really thinking of anything at all.

That exercise blew me away. Next, we tried it with our happiest memories, and we anchored to a different body part. And this is the story I chose to remember:

One summer afternoon, when I was about ten years old, I headed to my friend Graeme's house for a swim. His family had an old above-ground pool, nothing flash but I couldn't care less—it was a pool!

A few of the neighbourhood kids were splashing around with us, and after awhile we decided to have a race, boys versus girls. The pool was only around eight meters long, so we ran it like a relay race. I swam two laps first, then Graeme would bring us home strong for the win. It was *imperative* that we beat these girls, and we were fired up and READY.

On your mark, get set, GO! Off I went: I powered through that water like an Olympic athlete, kicking my legs 'till they burned, and

The Happy Bricklayer
Mark Bayer

when I got to the end I was in the lead. I pushed off the far wall with all my might and surged back towards Graeme. With precise timing, Graeme pushed off and began his lap. He was a superior swimmer to all of us and as he approached the final turn it was obvious we were winning.

I was cheering on Graeme for the win when he turned and gave an almighty push off the far end to begin his surge home, but that push was enough to tear a huge hole in the pool wall. As I stood there, mouth wide open in disbelief, the whole end of the pool collapsed and oceans of water came surging out onto the lawn. Poor bugger, Graeme had no idea. Still throwing his arms at break-neck speed, swimming for an epic win, unaware of the atrocity unfolding behind him, Graeme was sucked right out the arse end of the pool. He ended up lying on his stomach on his flooded backyard lawn.

It is the single funniest image I have ever seen with my own eyes. Even writing this memory I've been laughing out loud at the picture of Graeme swimming for gold whilst being sucked backwards out onto the grass. Actually, come to think of it, does that count as a win for the boys?

Right, back to the anchoring. So we thought about our funny stories whilst squeezing a finger on the other hand. Same result: when I cleared my mind and squeezed that finger, I immediately started bubbling over with happiness and laughter. (I suppose this

The Happy Bricklayer
Mark Bayer

might say something bad about me, taking pleasure from another's bad luck? But this bricklayer doesn't want to think too much about that.)

So why am I telling you these long-ago memories? Because there's an important lesson there! I was able to learn from that weekend course that a simple way to improve my mood is to just *remember happy memories.* Throughout my life, I keep coming up against these lessons about positive thoughts: *The Secret* taught me to ignore the negative self-talk about my job, and now I'd learned another tool for happiness. By just recalling a happy memory, I could instantly feel better.

Another tool I've learned to overcome symptoms of anxiety is a cold shock. For example, if you're waking in the morning and have anxious feelings about the day, splash your face with cold water or have a cold shower. The cold shock makes your body respond by increasing endorphins, the feel-good hormones in your brain, and eases those symptoms of anxiety. Cold water may also decrease cortisol, the stress-inducing hormone, and even just the shock takes your mind off things. Sometimes it's best just to snap the hell out of it!

The Happy Bricklayer
Mark Bayer

Deep thoughts for you to ponder:
- Memories have powerful emotions attached to them.
- Recalling funny memories is an immediate way to remove feelings of sadness.
- Hypnotherapy is great way to overcome addictions.

Cold water therapy can also be used by placing a sleeping friend's hand in cold water

The Happy Bricklayer
Mark Bayer

BRICK NINE: Changing Your Mind

Have you ever tried Hypnosis?
If not, why not?

The Happy Bricklayer
Mark Bayer

What is the funniest memory you can recall from your entire life?

How does it make you feel?

The Happy Bricklayer
Mark Bayer

Which celebrity would you like to hypnotise into thinking they were a bricklayer?

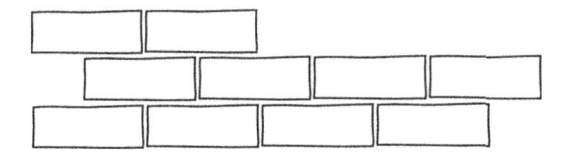

10. Getting Help

When I was studying life coaching, one thing I learned was that people rarely need to focus on just one goal. Usually there are multiple goals to work on simultaneously, and they're always interlinked.

For me, it's always been my job that has caused me the most unhappiness. But that wasn't my only problem, far from it. I've been overweight and had problems with my diet for as long as I can remember. I love my food and I get great pleasure from cooking and enjoying different meals—so I tend to eat too much, and too much of the wrong foods. I do a vegetable lasagne to die for, but my absolute favourite food is German, I do love a good sausage!

Over the years, I've tried dozens of diets and exercise programmes to lose weight, but nothing ever kept off the kilos. My weight has yo-yoed since childhood. Even after running a marathon I still couldn't stick to a healthy diet. So, three years ago I decided to find some outside help. The first thing I needed to quit was energy drinks. I never liked coffee, and I'd been addicted to high-caffeine energy drinks for over a decade. I knew how bad they were for me,

The Happy Bricklayer
Mark Bayer

and I'd tried to quit dozens of times. Then I'd have a bad night's sleep or some other trigger, and right away I'd relapse.

One day, I was working on a building site with a friend who was a smoker, and we got to talking about quitting. He said he'd quit for a year, but took it up again after separating from his wife. Now, this guy smoked more than a chimney, and I was impressed he'd managed a year off the ciggies. I asked him how he'd done it. "Hypnotism," he told me. "Paid a lady $300 and I quit on the spot."

That got me thinking. Well, I'd been impressed with the hypnotherapy course I did, and now I was a believer. So, I started to Google hypnotherapists in my area. Lo and behold, there was a lady with a practice not one hundred meters from my house! Well, that was too close to home. I couldn't ignore a hypnotherapist on my door step, could I?

It turned out this lady's name was Lauren (yes, *that* Lauren!), and she had amazingly positive reviews online—so I made a booking. After a 20 minute chat over the phone, she quoted me a 3-hour session—a huge amount of time for quitting energy drinks! But I was committed, so a few weeks later we met in her practice.

Lauren explained to me that hypnotherapy alone wasn't the best way to get lasting results. Instead, she preferred to get to the root of the problem. Then she started pelting me with questions,

The Happy Bricklayer
Mark Bayer

trying to get me to unlock when I was having the energy drinks, and WHY I would reach for them. How did drinking them make me feel?

I told her that each morning, as soon as I left home, I would drive to a service station for my first fix, and guzzle it down immediately. The drink would temporarily make me feel positive and happy. Then I'd have another at midday. I didn't have them on weekends, like most people with their daily coffee; I would only have them when working.

Lauren's reply to this floored me. She explained that it wasn't about feeling thirsty or needing some energy. I drank those drinks because I was going to a job I hated.

This was a revelation. My whole life, I had been using food to deal with stress and anxiety. Even now with my children, I used food as a reward. Being overweight made me want to eat for comfort, which gave me low self-esteem, which just made me eat more. It was an endless cycle, and now I was passing on my own bad habits to my kids.

Lauren taught me that all addictions are similar, whether it's food, alcohol, drugs, cigarettes or even exercise. If we want to break the bad habit, we first have to work on the reason we're triggered to do it. She explained that unless I made a change with my job, I would end up relapsing again. This was why we needed a three-hour session.

The Happy Bricklayer
Mark Bayer

For the next hour, we discussed my whole life and career. I told her of all my attempts at new business ideas, working overseas, life coaching and so on. She helped me see that just like the energy drinks, these attempts at change were different versions of me trying to escape bricklaying. And the reason why none of them was a success? None of them filled my sense of purpose.

When she asked me what I would eventually do with my life when I had a passive income that allowed me to stop doing bricklaying or building work, the answer was always the same: write my stories.

It was Lauren who challenged me that writing COULD be a career. Since I'd mastered bricklaying, she argued, why couldn't I do the same with writing? Without forcing me, she helped me find a compromise that I was comfortable with going forward. I wasn't willing to completely give up my income, but by working part time in construction I could dedicate lots of time to writing. I was confident that my family would approve of this too.

We finished our hypnotherapy session, and that's when I made changes to my work life, switching to part-time work so I could concentrate on writing. And you know what? I also quit drinking energy drinks. So far, it's been two years and I haven't had a single one—they just aren't an option anymore. That's impressive, considering they were my daily ritual for over a decade.

The Happy Bricklayer
Mark Bayer

Talking about bad habits, let me tell you a story from my time in London. One morning we were on our tea break at work: the usual mix of British foreman and tradesman, Polish labourers, and me, the Aussie brickie. There were always a few newspapers lying around for us to share. Everyone had a football team to read about, gossip to keep up on, and a Page 3 girl to ogle—not much talk of politics or world affairs on building sites!

That day, one of the guys snorted with laughter at a small article in *The Sun,* and he proceeded to read it out loud.

It seems a local cockney workman forgot his wallet at a building site, so he went back to collect it. He was in luck: a Polish labourer was in charge of locking up the site each day, and he was still there. But when the cockney opened the door to the change room, he found the Polish labourer in there alone, his pants around his ankles and a switched-on vacuum cleaner hose in his hand.

As you can imagine, both men got quite a fright! The Pole quickly dropped the vacuum and yanked up his pants. He proceeded to explain that it was tradition in his country to travel home from work clean, and he was just vacuuming the dust out of his underwear before his journey on public transport.

Do you believe that? Me neither. I think our friend the Pole had a bit of a bad habit going. I mean: pleasure yourself how you like mate, just don't use the work vac to do it.

The Happy Bricklayer
Mark Bayer

Right, back to addictions! As with our friend the Polish labourer, bad habits can be hard to break. If you're sneaking off to eat bad food, or waiting till everyone is in bed and having a drink of spirits or a quick ciggie (or if you're doing unspeakable things with a vacuum cleaner!), you know you shouldn't. You feel guilty, but I get it: the addiction is strong and hard to break. However, it's crucial to overcome your addictions so you are able to move towards your goals.

Whatever the addiction is you're holding on to, it has a control over you that is stopping you from starting your journey to your dream life. Addictions make you think you depend on them to make you happy, but that's not true. They cost money that could go towards achieving your goal. They cause your health to suffer, making it difficult to find the energy to make a positive change.

Being truly honest with ourselves and admitting our flaws is a huge step. Acknowledging our barriers and working out a plan to overcome our bad habits has to happen before we can begin to advance towards our dream lives.

Even before we lay the foundations or lay our first bricks for our dream home, we first we have to demolish the old dwelling. When we get help and overcome an addiction we free up time, money, and energy resources, reducing stress and putting us in a great head space to start building towards our goals, brick by brick.

The Happy Bricklayer
Mark Bayer

Habits are formed early in our lives—some good, some bad. As we become adults they become automatic. Getting up and going to work gets to be almost robotic. Eve when we've had a late night, our body clock wakes us at the right time. How many times have you woken up and it's only a minute before your alarm clock goes off?

When it comes to breaking a bad habit, freedom can seem impossible. Your body and mind are probably on autopilot, doing it without even thinking about it.

If you have a lifetime of habits making it tough to build your perfect life, I feel your pain. Like the saga of the energy drinks, I've had to break plenty of difficult habits.

Most new habits can be formed in a 2 to 4-week period. So straightaway, I think that's not a long a period to have to battle through. For example, instead of focusing on quitting cigarettes or alcohol or even sugar, just do it two weeks at a time. Give yourself a 2-week plan to get you through that first, most difficult period. Remove all triggers that are likely to make you want to indulge in the habit you're trying to break.

When I was trying to quit sugary treats, I noticed there were particular times when I would buy them. When refuelling my car, I would ALWAYS buy sweets. I would offer to refuel my wife's car for her so I could buy even more snacks! She was thinking I was being a

The Happy Bricklayer
Mark Bayer

kind husband, but I was just hooked—and finding any excuse to get my fix.

Now, each time I refuel, there's a visualisation exercise I do. I picture myself going into the service station and walking straight to the cashier, avoiding all the tempting products—and that just becomes the reality.

Remember that: *visualisation*.

The single most powerful tool you will get from any self-help book is visualisation. Remember the law of attraction? It's essentially the same thing, just picturing yourself doing what you want to do. You can use visualisation with your big life goals, but also with new habits you wish to form.

A huge part of your daily routine should be visualizing your dream life. You want to imagine different milestones along the way, and each time you revisit those thoughts, the details will sharpen and your imagination will get more vivid.

To really increase your chances of success, it's crucial to imagine the *feelings* you will have when you have reached your goal. Imagine it all: the positive energy you'll have, the happiness, contentment and euphoria you'll feel while living your dream life. Each milestone you pass on your brick-by-brick journey will have that feeling of excitement, and remember: the journey is part of attaining your goal so you will feel awesome along the way.

The Happy Bricklayer
Mark Bayer

The amazing thing about having these positive feelings is that they are like a magnet, and they'll attract more of those feelings. You'll begin to feel that positive energy more often, and that will reinforce you to keep using your visualisation, knowing that you are definitely on the right path.

That's why removing negative thoughts is so important: they will only attract more of the same. Get in the habit of eliminating them as quickly as possible and replacing them with positive thoughts of you living your dream life. Like any skill, the more you practice, the better you will become at it.

Another way of overcoming a bad habit is to replace the bad habit with a new healthy habit. I have a close friend who recently decided to quit drinking alcohol. I never thought of him as a big drinker, but he explained to me that he was drinking EVERY DAY and he was doing it as a way of coping with stress. He booked himself in with Lauren, and as her practice is so close to my house, he came over straight after for a visit.

He was super positive about taking the step. He was sure he wouldn't drink again and he could visualise all the positive things that would improve in his life. He'd have better sleeping quality, he'd feel less foggy, and have more focus in his day. His relationship with his wife and kids would improve. He'd have more money, too, since he'd probably save over a $100 a week not buying alcohol.

The Happy Bricklayer
Mark Bayer

I rang him a week later to see how he was going. I told him that he was already half way through the hardest part of forming new habits, that two-week period. He had joined a gym and he was enjoying the new facilities. He could easily afford the membership with the money saved from not buying booze. His family were happy for him to take the personal time to exercise as they were so proud of him quitting the drink. He even spent time with some friends whilst they were drinking, and he admitted it was challenging, but he felt so great for getting through it.

If you need help with an addiction I highly recommend seeking professional help. I've had great success with therapy and hypnotherapy, and I have some friends who've changed their lives around, too. (Though they still won't book me for a life coaching lesson.)

The Happy Bricklayer
Mark Bayer

Deep thoughts for you to ponder:

- Change isn't easy but it's necessary!
- Einstein said "The definition of insanity is doing the same thing over and over and expecting different results."
- Be on the lookout for moments of serendipity! Don't ignore them.
- Get advice from people who have had success with your goal.
- Hypnotherapy is a great tool to overcome bad habits.
- Replace a bad habit with a new positive one.
- Use a goal to help stay on track with your new habit.
- Exercise releases endorphins and is a great way of replacing a bad habit.
- You're never too old to start, or too young!

For the fellas, asking for help is like asking for directions, admitting you need help, but gets you to where you want to be.

The Happy Bricklayer
Mark Bayer

BRICK TEN: Breaking Bad Habits

What would be the bad habit you would like to change with hypnotherapy?
What is the trigger behind your bad habit?

The Happy Bricklayer
Mark Bayer

Is there a change you can make that will help you to break the bad habit?

What good habit could you replace the bad habit with?

The Happy Bricklayer
Mark Bayer

Have you ever had a moment of coincidence? A serendipitous meeting?

Is there someone you know who could help you?

The Happy Bricklayer
Mark Bayer

> Is your bad habit is stealing ladies underwear from strangers washing lines? I suggest choose a therapist that doesn't live or work anywhere near your house.

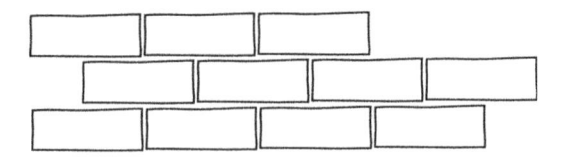

11. The TV Diet

One of my suggestions to kick-start new habits is the Happy Bricklayer's TV Diet.™ If you want to change your career and you can't afford to take time off work to start studying or training towards your dream job, then you have to find some TIME. Personally, my biggest timewasters are TV and playing on my phone.

How often do you sit down, pick up your phone and piss away an hour or two? Smart phones are super addictive: they're designed that way. Social media, games, messaging your mates—the list goes on. Just go on your phone right now and check your average screen time. Then add that to the time you spend sacked out in front of the TV each night.

Scary, right?

If you're genuinely serious about making a change, give the TV Diet a try. You can go cold turkey if you like, but it might be more realistic to cut down. Instead of two hours of TV a night, try one hour twice a week. Even if you just do that on weekdays, you've freed up EIGHT HOURS to spend working towards your dream life.

The Happy Bricklayer
Mark Bayer

My first experience with the TV Diet was purely accidental. Belinda and I had moved to London and left behind the house we'd just built, so we didn't have to work nights and weekends on the construction site. We rented a furnished one-bedroom apartment in Earls Court. Now in Australia, rentals come without furniture, but in England they're mostly furnished—except no TV. Well, as we were only going to be there short term, we had no intention of buying a TV and having to sell it later. So, we just decided to go without one.

That time without a television was the best six months of our lives. *(Sorry kids! It was before you were born, you pair of handbrakes!* 😄 *)*

What a revelation it was! It was the beginning of spring and the nights were getting longer, so Belinda and I would meet at home after work and we'd go for a walk. We could walk to Hyde Park in twenty minutes, to the free museums in South Kensington in thirty minutes. Notting Hill, Chelsea, Fulham, and even Buckingham Palace were within walking distance! We would get dinner at a pub a few times a week for five pounds each and when it was dark we would read at home. I didn't miss TV one bit! We had a video store nearby and we'd occasionally rent a movie and watch it on our laptop. But we loved being out and about so much, the TV wasn't even missed.

It was also the first time since high school that I started writing. Ideas had been flooding my mind for years, and I'd started

The Happy Bricklayer
Mark Bayer

reading about how to write screen plays. Soon I started jotting down little scenarios and movie scenes in my spare time.

Six months later, we moved into a share house with a TV, and as it was winter we tended to be inside a lot more. Soon enough, we were back in front of the box. But that first six months in London without a TV were pure bliss. If you truly decide to go after your dream, then cutting out TV is the best way to free up some time.

Same deal with your phone. You can easily add screen time limiters on it, so you get reprimanded by your device when you're on it too long. Plan your life around your goals! Then allow yourself to have screen time once you've done your study or training.

Another idea is to remove social media from your phone completely. You can still access it from your laptop, but you won't spend endless hours scrolling through that handheld screen. It's surprising how much time can disappear when you pick up your phone and check social media. Remove that possibility and use your free time to work on your goal!

The tv diet is a game changer when it comes to a career change. Most of us looking to change careers will need time to study or time to train towards our new professions. You might be starting your own business, and initially you still have to work full time and fit in your goal in around your work hours. Start by keeping a log of your day to find out where you can find that extra time. I guarantee

The Happy Bricklayer
Mark Bayer

you will be shocked at just how much time in a seven-day week you will spend on your phone and in front of the TV.

There are so many options you can try! For example I love to watch sports. I'm a huge Chelsea FC supporter in the English Premier League, and in Australia I support the Cronulla Sharks in the NRL. I watch basketball, cricket and some boxing, even darts and tennis—the list goes on! This could amount to a huge time suck—except for one thing.

Most of the sport I now watch on my phone whilst on a treadmill at the gym. I like to run to keep fit, even though I don't have the physique for running. Truth be told, I'm built like a brick shit house, made for lifting heavy things, not running. But I have found over the years that managing my weight with cardio and running a few race events every year gives me motivation. And I do all my training on a treadmill.

People often tell me to run outside, but honestly, it's where I get to watch all my sport. If I do four runs a week, that's four hours of sport I can watch. Plus, we're so lucky that we're in this age of technology so I can now watch a condensed version of each match instead of the whole 90 minutes. I can catch up on all my favourite teams and get my exercise in, all at the same time!

Over to you—where you can save time to add bricks to your dream life build?

The Happy Bricklayer
Mark Bayer

> Deep thoughts for you to ponder:
>
> - Keep a diary for a week to record exactly how much time you spend on devices and TV to help you cut back.
> - Keeping a daily log will limit wasted time and help find time to allocate towards working on your goal.
> - Removing social media accounts and games from your phone removes the temptation to waste time.

A bloke multi-tasking, who'd have thought? Right?

The Happy Bricklayer
Mark Bayer

BRICK ELEVEN: Finding The Time

What are your priorities, working on your goals or watching reruns of "Friends?"
Can you multi task and get your TV fix whilst exercising?

The Happy Bricklayer
Mark Bayer

Have you ever tried going cold turkey on TV? Try a month! (NoTVember?)

Who do you think would have the sexiest voice to do the audio book for 'The Happy Bricklayer?'

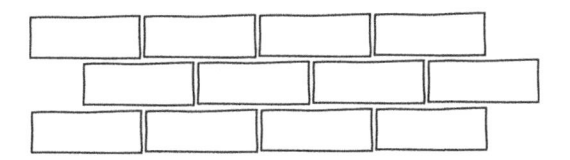

12. Our Belief Systems Are Learned In Our Childhoods

Guilt had been holding me back from chasing my dream. Mostly, my guilt was centred around my relentless need to provide for my family. Growing up, my father was the sole bread winner, while my mum kept the loveliest and tidiest home on the planet. Mum never sat still. She would clean the whole house from top to bottom, the gardens were immaculate, and dinner was five stars every night. But my dad provided financially, and he worked hard and long hours in construction. Like myself, he had no love of his job.

So much of our belief systems are learned in our childhoods. By watching my father growing up, I learned that being the man of the house meant working hard, even if you got no pleasure from your job. As a father, I believed I had to do the same. But why? My wife has a great job and she earns a good income. Why do I still feel guilty about not providing for my family?

Every one of us has a different relationship with money. We all earn different amounts, save different amounts, spend different amounts, and form our own opinion on how we should treat it.

The Happy Bricklayer
Mark Bayer

The first place we learn about money is from our parents. We see how they budget and spend. For example, even though my dad was a hard worker and provided well for the five of us, it was my mum who balanced the books and managed to scrimp and save.

My father was not a risk-taker by any means. If he wanted something, he wouldn't draw down his savings or buy it on credit; he would work harder or more hours to pay for it in cash.

When I started working, I followed in my dad's footsteps. If I wanted something I was willing to work hard for it, and I took on extra jobs to save faster. At 14, I got my first job working at a chemist, delivering prescription medicine to elderly people in the neighbourhood.

From my first payday I was hooked. That feeling of spending my own money on whatever I wanted was addictive. Each week, I spent a little of my money on frivolous things, but I always saved half of it or more. My mum deposited my savings in the bank, and I loved to see my balance grow.

Soon I was saving for bigger items: a stereo, a new wetsuit, and new albums and cassettes (how we dinosaurs listened to music in the '80s.) After a few years I got a new job cleaning horse stables from 5- 7 AM before school, Monday to Friday. I actually quite liked the work. It was great money and I was learning to work with the beautiful animals. But in hindsight, it was a disaster for my schooling.

The Happy Bricklayer
Mark Bayer

Before my job with the horses, I'd always been an above average student—even though I was a bit lazy with homework. But now I was headed into my last two years of high school and waking up in the dark every day. I was tired all the time and my grades began to suffer.

At the time my parents were so proud of my work ethic that they didn't consider any of the negatives. I was learning the importance of hard work, and I was saving up for a car— so they saw no problem.

Now I look back on those first experiences earning money and I have a very different opinion. I wouldn't say I was wrong to to work hard, or that my parents were wrong to encourage me. But a decade later, I realized there was a whole other way to do things.

One of my first accountants, a sharp woman named Filomena, told me how she dealt with money for her kids. Her son was at university, and he wanted money for socializing. So she made a deal with him. She didn't want him to work, so she paid him to study. He had to commit to a schedule, and be in his room on time— just like a job. In return, she'd pay him to study, and he had to pass his exams as part of the deal.

Filomena gave him a car to use and spending money, enough to keep up his social commitments and nothing more. At first, it sounded to me like she was spoiling him. But she explained it

The Happy Bricklayer
Mark Bayer

differently: she said it was an investment in his future. After his classes, there were only so many hours in the day, and if he was working as well as spending time with friends, she knew that study time would be last on his list of priorities.

I have to agree. It definitely wouldn't work for everyone, but I wonder if I would have kept my grades up if I'd been given the same money NOT to work at the horse stables. As it was, I ended up dropping out of school to avoid the inevitable poor results in my final exams.

My wife Belinda also learned her money habits in childhood. She's a much better saver than me. She spends very little money on herself, and she isn't interested in extravagant indulgences. She gets this from her father, who's very shrewd with money since he grew up poor. By the time I met him, he had five properties and investments in the stock market but we could only go for dinner at "The Black Stump" because he knew we could get a discount with a coupon.

When Belinda and I moved in together and started sharing money, it was quite the learning curve for me. She taught me that it's easier to save a dollar than earn it. Like her father, she would do her five-day, 38-hour working week, then spend her money only on essentials. By contrast, I was working six days and 50+ hours a week—but on my day off, I treated us to bottles of wine and

The Happy Bricklayer
Mark Bayer

restaurant meals, feeling I had earned the privilege. And at the end of the week, Belinda was saving as much as me.

When you think about the obstacles in place that are keeping you from building a happy life, is money at the top of the list? Then maybe you should take a look not just at how you're earning it, but also how you're spending and saving. Personally, when I started looking at things from a different perspective, I made VERY different choices.

Back to that first accountant Filomena, the one who paid her grown son to study. I was talking to her about selling my house and buying a cheaper one. I explained we were trying for a family, interest rates were high, and our expenses would use up all of my income whilst Belinda wasn't working.

To my surprise, Filomena shook her head. "Don't sell," she told me. "Increase the mortgage on your house, so you can take out some cash as a cushion."

"Are you insane?" I answered (though it's possible I spoke more politely than that.) "Our payments will increase! That's taking a step backwards!"

"No, it isn't." Filomena took out her notepad and showed me the figures. "You see, once Belinda stops working, you'll be going $150 into the red each week. If you borrow that money against your house, you can cover the extra expense. Meanwhile, your property

The Happy Bricklayer
Mark Bayer

will continue to accrue in value, and you can avoid all the stress and expense of moving house. It's good debt, actually."

Good debt? It was the first time in my life I'd considered such a thing. I was so used to saving something every week, no matter what, that I couldn't imagine losing money, even if it was only temporary. Then she explained that after a year Belinda would be back at work part time and we would be covering our expenses then.

Look, we're all stuck in the programming we learned in our childhoods. That's why it's important to get multiple opinions, especially when it comes to money. If I hadn't talked to Filomena, I might have sold the house—a terrible financial decision.

One night back in London, my roommate Jarrod asked for my advice about money. Belinda and I owned (with a mortgage) our house in Sydney, and he wanted to know how we were able to save the deposit for it.

I explained that we both worked full-time and rented in a cheaper area for a year to help save, but mostly I worked Saturdays, and that made all the difference. By working one extra day a week, I was able to double my savings. Not to mention, I had to stay in on Friday nights instead of partying, so my expenses went down too. By working 20% more, I was saving *more than twice as much.*

Jarrod was inspired, so I hired him to work with me the next Saturday. Now this guy was about 60kg dripping wet, and I had him

The Happy Bricklayer
Mark Bayer

carrying boxes of tiles up four flights of stairs. After about half an hour he stopped talking, and by lunchtime he was exhausted. I have never seen anyone devour a foot-long subway sandwich as quickly as he did. He worked for six hours that Saturday and earned the equivalent of two days' wages on his full-time job, but he never asked to come back again. Ah, well, hard work—it's not be for everyone!

In my current situation, I'm doing pretty much the opposite with my work hours. I'm working part-time so I can spend time concentrating on my writing, and I'm not wasting mental energy going mad with too much construction work. Every stage of your journey is different, and it's okay to adapt to what's most important to you at the time. If I hadn't put in the hard work in my twenties and thirties, then it would be harder to afford the time off I'm taking now.

Sure, Happy Bricklayer, good on ya, I can hear you say. *But what about those of us who DON'T have a paid-off house and passive investments?*

What if you want to change jobs but you're renting and you have no savings? Is it even possible to take the leap? The answer is YES. Anything is possible. If you really want to change, you just have to find a way. There is so much information out there on budgeting and ways to save money. There are always new ways of moving forward, and money is NOT a reason to give up your dreams.

The Happy Bricklayer
Mark Bayer

We live in a time when we have so much pressure to have EVERYTHING, but happiness isn't something you can buy. It feels great to drive an expensive sports car and have a mansion on the beach—but will those things make you *happy*? I can promise you, if you have to work 60 hours a week in a job you despise to get those riches, those fancy toys won't make you happy at all.

And you know what you can't buy? Time.

Let me tell you a little story about time. I've coached my son Ewan's soccer team now for six years, and I remember our first-ever game when the boys were in kindergarten. It was an away game and I was just grabbing the gear, a kit bag and a sack of balls. A few of the boys' mums approached and offered to help me with the equipment.

"Sure," I said. "Can one of you just grab my ball sack?"

Shit, that was awkward. I can't remember if we won or lost that game, but we all remember that comment.

At first, I was reluctant to volunteer on the team. I never played soccer growing up, and I didn't have very much experience. But none of the other parents were willing to sacrifice one night a week and every Saturday morning to games and training, so here we are. At times it feels like a stitch up, a free child-minding service. Parents drop off and pick up, most don't want to stay and join in, and I guess that's fair enough. They might have other kids, and we're all

The Happy Bricklayer
Mark Bayer

busy, I get it. But after six years, some of these boys have never had their dad come to a single game or training session.

I find that mind-blowing. I love watching my son play and being involved in his team. I'm sure he sometimes finds it frustrating to have his dad as the coach, and maybe I lean on him more than the others—but mostly, he's positive about it. Not only do I get time with him, I have a close relationship with all his friends because I'm their coach. They all chat with me at school when I see them, and I'm a part of their world. What a privilege that is! When they muck about and I get frustrated, I remind myself how lucky I am.

And here's why I'm blathering on about my son's soccer team: providing for my family has always been important to me, but quality time with my kids is my priority. We all have our own standards as to the amount of quality time we spend with family, and that's great. But when my wife wanted to return to work a year after our kids were born, I made the best choice of my life: I started taking one day a week off work.

It started when my daughter was 15 months old. It had taken us seven years to fall pregnant, so we were a little over-protective with her. But Belinda wanted to keep her work skills up-to-date, and began working on Fridays, just one day a week. I talked to my business partner Rado, and he was okay with it. So, my four-day

The Happy Bricklayer
Mark Bayer

week started. I still worked the occasional Saturdays, but Daddy Day-care Fridays was born.

It was the best. My gorgeous little girl Bella and I would play and cuddle, read books, go to the park, and just spend every moment together. We are super-close to this day, and I'm sure our connection was forged during those years of Daddy Day-care Fridays. When we first started, if she fell over or hurt herself she would always call out for Mummy. It was her automatic reaction, as Mum had ALWAYS been there. But as time went on, she learned that Dad was there for her, too.

Years later, when Belinda returned to work after having our son Ewan, I did it again, taking every Friday off work to spend time with the kids. We would go to the city and see the aquarium or the zoo; we'd go to the beach—it was just the best bonding time ever. I did that for years until they started pre-school, and I'm so proud of myself for choosing those Fridays instead of the extra money.

The Happy Bricklayer
Mark Bayer

Deep thoughts for you to ponder:

- We learn our spending and saving habits from our parents.
- Working long hours can damage other areas of your life
- Only you can decide what work-life balance is best for you
- One thing you can't buy is…time.

Like sands through the hour glass, so are the lectures from our wives

The Happy Bricklayer
Mark Bayer

BRICK TWELVE: Bad Habits Are Learned Early

Who did you learn your money habits from?
Where do you think you could improve your spending habits?

The Happy Bricklayer
Mark Bayer

Do you budget your money every week?

Is living your dream life more important than money?

The Happy Bricklayer
Mark Bayer

> What totally annoying habit do you hope to pass on to your children?

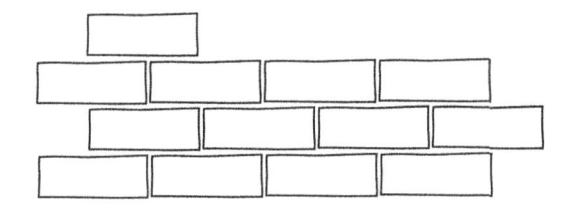

13. Money

Ah, that necessary evil! The greatest challenge you will encounter when changing careers is the financial worries. Part of the reason it took me over 25 years was that I thought I wasn't in a financial position to allow myself the time off work to write. To be honest though, I could have changed much sooner if I'd known how.

The truth is, we spend a lot of time considering the worst-case scenarios instead of focusing on the huge possibilities. I could have asked my wife Belinda to start full-time work years earlier. I could have driven my car for another few years instead of upgrading it. We could have holidayed in a caravan park up the coast instead of going overseas. It comes down to making that commitment to yourself, sticking to your plan, and *never giving up*.

This book isn't just for those who can afford the time and money to study or retrain. Not everyone has a spouse to take up the slack. Not everyone owns their own home or has a passive income.

But if you truly desire it, there's always a way. It will take dedication and sacrifice to make it happen, but once you know this

The Happy Bricklayer
Mark Bayer

change will lead to you living your dream life, then all the hard work will be worth it.

Careful planning means planning out each step toward your goal, brick by brick. You will work out all the costs involved work out a budget around those costs. Can you afford any time off work to spend studying or training? Can you change your work hours to get a higher pay, such as working the night shift? Maybe you can cut costs by moving in with family or a friend. Can you sell your car and use public transport? Perhaps your spouse is happy to increase their work hours to see you achieve your dream. Unless you ask, you won't know. It may seem a little selfish, but surely living your dream life is the one indulgence worth asking for help to achieve. I can assure you that once you start on the journey, those who are closest to you will see your new demeanour, and they won't regret helping you. Because in the end, you being happy makes *their* lives better. Who knows, maybe you'll inspire them to make a change too.

(Just remember to buy them a copy of this book! You NEED your copy actually—be sure to use a pen and not a pencil when writing your answers to the questions at the end of each chapter—see? Now you can't lend it out!)

I can guarantee you this: for every reason you can come up with not to start this journey, there are several solutions that will help you overcome that barrier. Whenever you feel dejected, keep your dream life in mind. Visualise yourself living that awesome new life every day. Hold in your mind's eye a life that gives you satisfaction and fulfillment, and you will constantly find new ways to overcome the hurdles that pop up along the way.

No matter your situation, you have the ability to change. And believe me, as soon as you start you'll get a taste of that feeling I'm talking about. With every brick you lay, you will see your dream life being built. Little by little, it will become a reality—and that feeling will become addictive, and spur you to keep adding bricks till you finish building your dream life.

If you need help for budgeting there are many sources of free information available. In Australia there is a government web page called Moneysmart, I have friends who got a lot out of the "Barefoot Investor" who uses multiple bank accounts with direct debits to allocate money for bills and helps with budgeting. There are websites to help with coupons to get discounts, Debt angels if you need help to get on top of mounting debt, and many other ways of managing money. A thorough plan of your finances will help you plan your brick by brick blue print and is integral to guaranteeing your plan is accurate and realistic.

The Happy Bricklayer
Mark Bayer

> ## Deep thoughts for you to ponder:
>
> - You don't need as much money as you think to get by.
> - There are plenty of options to cut back expenses.
> - Focus on solutions, not obstacles.

You can always become the tight arse of your social group to save a few bucks, but that role is usually already taken, right?

The Happy Bricklayer
Mark Bayer

BRICK THIRTEEN: Money, Money, Money!

How can you cut expenses to help you afford more time to work on your goals?

Who can help you manage your finances?

The Happy Bricklayer
Mark Bayer

What unnecessary expenses can you go without?
How much do you get for a second hand soul these days?

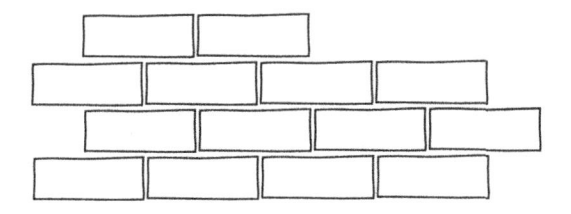

14. Masonry Technician

I have friends who don't quite understand why I would take such a big financial loss by giving up full-time work, or by taking all school holidays off and having twelve-week holidays instead of the usual four.

And for a long time, I felt the need to justify my decisions. I'd take pains to explain my reasoning, telling them I wasn't enjoying my work and I wanted to spend more time with my kids. And when we disagreed on our lifestyle goals I would then have negative thoughts about my friends. *Oh, they don't spend enough time with their kids. Pity, they value things more than experience. Why do they work 50 hours a week in that job they don't like?*

What I learned is that I was judging THEM. To truly follow my heart and live my ideal life, I needed to stop judging. Because when I'm judging others, I'm also worried about people judging me. My ideal life won't look the same as anyone else's ideal life. The amount of time I want to spend with my family will be different to what others

The Happy Bricklayer
Mark Bayer

determine is right for them. How they feel about their job will be different to how I feel about mine.

I now try really hard to push those thoughts from my head, though it can be difficult at times. All around us, we see people making it big on social media: buying new cars, going on exotic holidays, and we're bombarded by stories in the media about the rich and famous. It's not easy to stop judging others, and it's even harder to stop judging ourselves.

My worst self-judging was with my job title. I felt embarrassed to introduce myself as a "bricklayer," because I thought people would judge me as an undesirable character. On job sites, we would call ourselves "Masonry Technicians" for a laugh, just because we felt there was so much stigma attached to being a bricklayer, and Masonry Technician sounded more professional.

This was particularly obvious with my kids. When they started school, I told them to tell their friends I was a builder, not a bricklayer. The kids were confused. They knew I was a bricklayer. They weren't embarrassed about it, so why should I be? I felt that people automatically judged me based on my profession, thinking I was oafish, dense and inadequate. But I've worked hard now to overcome that feeling. Even if people have a poor opinion of bricklayers, I don't give a shit. At least I'm not a crooked real estate agent! Ha-ha. Just kidding, no judging. Anyway, by writing my own

The Happy Bricklayer
Mark Bayer

book called *The Happy Bricklayer,* I guess I've finally overcome that issue. Any day now, millions (or dozens) of copies will be flooding stores around the world, and I could become the most famous bricklayer on the planet!

Here's what I've learned: when I notice the negative thoughts come into my head, I acknowledge them, then make the conscious decision to not judge. Finally, I remind myself that I'm on the right track for ME.

We all carry around a mental image of ourselves. That self-image reflects our actions, feelings, behaviour, and even our abilities. But the interesting thing is that we have the ability to CHANGE our self-image.

It's like we subconsciously give ourselves a rating out of ten and rank ourselves against others. Some of us might be overly harsh on ourselves, whereas we all know some guy who looks fairly average but thinks he sees Brad Pitt in the mirror.

I read a study once by a plastic surgeon who observed his patients' behaviour before and after their surgeries. One patient came in with a large nose that he was unhappy with and wanted to change.

This patient thought of himself as ugly, and this gave him a negative self-image. After the surgery however, the doctor saw an immediate psychological change. The patient was instantly happier

The Happy Bricklayer
Mark Bayer

because he now viewed himself as a much more attractive person, and his whole personality changed as his self-image was so much improved.

It shows that we all have an opinion of ourselves that limits our success. If we're able to improve our self-image, then our lives will get better to match our new expectations. (By the way, I'm not suggesting you should go get a nose job!)

All animals are born with a success mechanism that helps them survive. A squirrel has the instinct to collect nuts to survive the winter; a duck migrates with the seasons to find better resources. We humans, on the other hand, are the only ones who use our IMAGINATIONS to create goals. We can *direct our success mechanism* by using our imaginations.

Our built-in success mechanism needs a goal that we *believe exists* and we therefore know it is *possible to achieve*. When we're able to focus on what we look like once we've achieved our goal, the "how we got there" part will take care of itself.

We all make mistakes along the way. I certainly have, and I'm sure I'll make more in the future. But mistakes are the lessons that help us to correct as we move towards our goals. We learn new skills by trial and error, and eventually we learn the right way forward from each lesson.

The Happy Bricklayer
Mark Bayer

The best path forward is to use our imaginations to clearly see ourselves achieving our success. Hold a mental picture of yourself in your mind's eye, living your ideal life. The better the details in your imagination, the more your brain will believe it to be an actual experience. Imagine how you will feel when you finally achieve your goal. That feeling of success will help you strive to obtain that sensation.

Another part of your self-improvement journey should include learning to treat others kindly. Mental health is such a big issue in this modern world, and we should all endeavour to be kinder people. That includes the way we interact with friends and family, even work colleagues and strangers on the street.

It can be easy to throw biting comments at people for a laugh. I know better than anyone how much that happens with groups of men on a building site. I love a bit of banter more than most, but it's important to be aware you really have no idea how others are feeling inside.

That person you're teasing might have some major issues at home, or they might have a sick relative. They might be getting bullied elsewhere, and adding to it might push them over the edge. As it happens, I've experienced that one myself.

There was one time when my love of pranking went too far. I played a prank on my work mate Rado, and it could have been

The Happy Bricklayer
Mark Bayer

funny—but unbeknownst to me, three other people had the same idea.

It was early in my career, and I was about 22 years old. I got to the job site later in the day, as I'd had to finish a small job on another site first. When I arrived, everyone was in back doing an extension to an existing house, so they were couldn't see me rock up. *Ah, the perfect opportunity,* I thought. We'd all been pranking each other a lot in those days, so I seized my chance.

I jacked up the front wheels on Rado's little old rusty Suzuki Swift. I put bricks under the front axle, raising it high enough that the front wheels were half an inch off the ground. When he went to drive away, the wheels would just spin.

Happy with my trick, I went around back to join the guys. Meanwhile I had no idea that Rado had already been getting a hard time that day. He was the apprentice, and he felt he was being unfairly targeted. He was visibly upset.

We were closing in on lunch time when someone sneakily put mortar on the underside of Rado's trowel, a common bricklayer trick. As he gripped the trowel, the mortar squished all over the palm of his hand. That was it for Rado.

"Fuck off you bastards, I'd rather eat by myself." He climbed off the scaffold and stormed off to have his lunch break.

The Happy Bricklayer
Mark Bayer

Unfortunately, that was just the beginning. Rado grabbed his drink, a 2-litre bottle of grape juice. Someone had drilled a hole in the neck of the plastic bottle, and when he tipped back the bottle, a load of juice poured down his shirt front. Rado exploded. He threw the mostly full bottle into the concrete slab and screamed abuse at us all. Then he packed up his tools and announced he was going home.

At this point I was freaking out. I had no idea about all those other pranks. I was hoping I could convince him to stay and get the bricks out from under his axle before he found them. But Rado was beside himself with rage, not willing to be calmed. He marched out to his car.

At this point, all of the guys were feeling guilty. We followed him out to apologize and try and convince him to stay, but he wasn't having a bar of it. I watched in horror as he headed to his car. He opened the boot to put in his tools and bag and someone had filled his boot with a huge bale of hay.

He went the brightest shade of red I have ever seen.

He was screaming abuse at us all, but we couldn't help but laugh. It was just hilarious as all this poor guy wanted to do was leave and now he had to remove the bale of hay, loose bits falling everywhere, to finally put his tools in the car.

The Happy Bricklayer
Mark Bayer

Now, no one but me knew about the brick under the axle, so it was like watching a train wreck in slow motion for me. We all stood and watched as he finally tried to leave. He started the engine and released the hand brake, then the engine roared and the wheels spun at top speed. Rado sort of leaned forward, expecting the car to move, but his tyres were spinning in space.

It took him a few seconds to realize, and by now everyone was rolling on the floor in hysterics whilst I apologized profusely and rushed to my car to get the jack so I could take out the bricks. Poor Rado had fallen victim to no fewer than four separate pranks that day, though none of us had realized until it was too late. We were just trying to have fun, but to Rado it felt like a case of severe bullying. None of us was trying to make him feel bad! But that day, the stars just aligned against him.

He wouldn't talk to any of us for days. The boss sent him to another job site for a few weeks and gave us all a good telling off. It's a strange memory to recall, as 25 years later it's still one of the most hilarious things I have ever witnessed in my life, but I also feel a lot of shame because Rado felt so upset, bullied and angry.

Thankfully, I can tell you that Rado went on to become one of my closest friends. We worked together every day for two decades, and I've probably spent more time with him than I have with anyone else on this planet. He's the most trustworthy and

The Happy Bricklayer
Mark Bayer

generous person I've ever met. I'm so grateful he forgave me for that day.

Rado and I have had plenty of laughs at work since that day, but I waited a good few years to pull another prank. And I definitely don't go overboard. I can't take back that experience with Rado, but I can make sure I don't hurt someone like that again in the future. Respect.

The Happy Bricklayer
Mark Bayer

> ## Deep thoughts for you to ponder:
>
> - If you catch yourself judging someone in a negative way, even in your thoughts, stop and change your thoughts.
> - No matter what others think of you it actually makes zero difference—so who cares?
> - Any negative thoughts are a complete waste of time and energy. They help no one, so just let them go.
> - Comparing ourselves to others is really unhelpful. Focus on yourself and your loved ones.

Judging others is a total waste of time and energy, unless of course they are Manchester United supporters, then judge away those red sods.

BRICK FOURTEEN: Take A Look In The Mirror

Do you feel ashamed of your job?

Does judging yourself or others help you to move forward?

The Happy Bricklayer
Mark Bayer

How can you improve your self image?

What does your life look like when you are working in your dream job?

The Happy Bricklayer
Mark Bayer

How do you feel when you envisage you living your best life?
Have you ever pranked your best friend in public? If not, are they really your best friend?

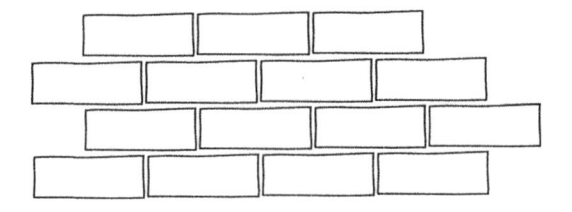

15. Timeline

When you're working on your goals, it's important to hold an image in your mind of the end result. One way of doing that is with a timeline, which will help you to visualise important milestones along the way. Like memories that have a strong emotion attached to them, by focusing on the milestones on the brick by brick construction of your new life, you will feel the positive feelings that come with achievement.

Suppose you have a job in retail, but you've always dreamt of having your own dog grooming business. The thought of having your own shop, a few employees, playing about with dogs every day and being your own boss fills you with such excitement that you're sure this new venture is the key to your happiness.

First, you'll need to work out the necessary steps to make it happen. You'll need to get training and practice with your grooming skills, and probably an official qualification. Next, you'll want to get a job working at someone else's dog grooming business, so you can get some experience while you save for your own. You should probably brush up on your business skills, so you might want to take a class there. And you'll need to write out a detailed business plan so you can approach a bank for a start-up loan.

Write those steps out. Get in as much detail as possible, and using a timeline for visualisation helps a great deal.

I live near the beach and I love using the sand for this exercise. First of all, a long walk on the beach frees up your mind and helps get you into a positive mind frame. Find a stick you can use to draw a long line in the sand, maybe five to ten metres long. Along the line, you can mark the milestones that you'll hit on your journey.

Back to the dog grooming dream. You decide it'll take one year of working in your current job and training in your spare time to get the qualification you need to be a licensed dog groomer. You stand on the line you've drawn in the sand, knowing you're at the beginning of the journey.

Now close your eyes and step forward one year along your timeline. Yes, actually *physically move your body* along your imaginary timeline.

You are now one year into the future. You've just finished your course and attained the qualification. What does it look like? Is your name in calligraphy? Is it framed? Are you excited? Are your family and friends there, congratulating you? Maybe you're looking healthier because you're spending your spare time practicing your

The Happy Bricklayer
Mark Bayer

grooming and not eating junk food in front of the TV! Imagine how good you're feeling as you've done exactly what you set out to do, in the exact timeframe you said you would do it.

Now step forward just a little bit. It's two months later and you just got your first-ever dog grooming job. Your interview went well and they called to offer you the position. You gave notice at your old job and you and your old work mates are out for a farewell dinner. They'll miss you, as you've been such a positive person to be around. (And it's no secret why! You were content at work knowing you were on your path to happiness.)

Step forward another year and see what you look like now. You've been the perfect employee, never missing a day, with a thirst to learn. Your boss adores you and she's asked you to run the business whilst she has maternity leave. You're now studying business after work, and learning how to manage will be great experience for you. The promotion has also helped you save for the start-up costs of your own business. Personally, your relationships with friends and family have never been better.

Another step forward in time. Another year on, and you've finished your course on small business. You're confident you now have the knowledge to successfully run your own enterprise. You've completed a thorough and detailed business plan, you've secured a business loan, and you're ready to look for your own premises. How

The Happy Bricklayer
Mark Bayer

do you feel at this moment? You've been hitting every single target you set yourself these past two years, which gives you so much confidence. Perhaps you could even buy the business off your boss! Anything is possible.

A small step forward now, three months. You've just completed your first week of business in your own grooming salon. You've set it up just the way you want it. You have the best equipment and you're in the perfect premises, with no nearby competition. The social media campaign you learned how to do on your business course was a smash success, and you've been flat out all week. You're already considering hiring an assistant!

This time, take a big step forward, projecting yourself five years further in the future. What does life look like? Perhaps you have several salons now and enjoy a balance of grooming and running your business. Or maybe you kept things simple and just love the hands-on grooming. Have you expanded the business, maybe started a boarding kennel? The world is your oyster! Imagine where you are, in as much detail as you can.

Using the timeline is such a great way to get clarity on your steps towards your goal. And you don't have to stop at just one! You can work on multiple goals at the same time. Like me, your health might have been suffering if you were treating your unhappiness with food, alcohol, cigarettes, or drugs. By working towards our

The Happy Bricklayer
Mark Bayer

sense of purpose, we are in a much better place to work on eliminating bad habits and replacing them with good ones, and it's easy to visualise these results on a timeline.

Deep thoughts for you to ponder:

- Timeline therapy is an amazing tool to design the brick-by-brick steps that will build your dream life.
- All goals need specific time restrictions to keep you focused and hitting your targets.

Drawing cock and balls on your friend's timeline is not helpful but do it anyway.

BRICK FIFTEEN: Mapping Out Your Dream

Do you have a beach where you can do your timeline? If not, where can you do it? Chalk on a driveway? Masking tape on a hallway?
What are the milestones you achieve when you walk your timeline into the future?

The Happy Bricklayer
Mark Bayer

What are the time frames for each of these milestones?

How will you know when you have laid all your bricks and finished building your dream life?

The Happy Bricklayer
Mark Bayer

> When you see yourself in the future living your dream life, how many copies of *The Happy Bricklayer* have you purchased for family and friends?

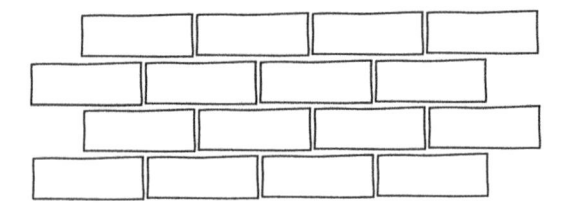

16.   Procrastination

One of my greatest challenges to overcome has been procrastination. My entire life I've been the type of person who leaves things until it's almost too late. In school all my studying and assignments were done in a blazing hot rush, all at the last minute. Of course, that had predictable results.

As an adult I've looked into this more, and I've found that I'm easily distracted, disorganized, I talk too much, and I often interrupt. Most of the time it's not a big problem for me, except for when I have to concentrate on tasks that I find boring.

Of course, most people struggle with uninteresting tasks. What's frustrating is when I put off things that I actually want to do.

For example, my goal right now is to not only finish some manuscripts, but to have them published and become a successful writer. So why is it that I find a thousand ways to distract myself from getting to the keyboard and finishing my drafts? Is it self-sabotage, or just laziness?

I'm not sure. But there is a cure.

The Happy Bricklayer
Mark Bayer

For me, it comes down to time management and routine. Let's face it, we all know what we need to do, but without deadlines we tend to put things off. I'm inspired by my friend Benny, who was once a national bodybuilding champion. He explained to me that when he was training towards his goal, he was so focused that he had a diary with every day broken down into 15-minute intervals.

He literally planned out every 15 minutes of every day and wrote down what he would do at all times. Bodybuilders train a lot, eat a lot, and he also needed to rest a lot. He actually quit his job and lived in a motor home, travelling 2,000 kilometres over two years as he worked towards his goal of becoming the national champion, driving from Mackay in North Queensland to Sydney. And every day of those two years, he broke his time into 15-minute intervals, and each of those intervals was a step towards his goal.

Was this nuts? To some, maybe.

Did he care? No.

And guess what? He did it. He won the national bodybuilding championship. And he did it because he planned every step of the way.

I remember how his girlfriend at the time, Cassandra (now his wife) would complain about him not spending enough time with her. He thought he was being generous by giving her two of his fifteen-minute time slots every day! Benny is a little full on, but he's

The Happy Bricklayer
Mark Bayer

also one of the most goal-driven and committed people I have ever met.

When you come across someone who has a quality you admire, try to find out more about them. How did they achieve their goals? That's what I learned from Benny. Maybe you don't want to plan your day down to every 15-minute interval, but if you set your goals precisely, you will find achieving them much simpler.

Another key part of achieving your goals is to lose the scepticism. Replace those negative thoughts with faith—and I don't mean the God kind. As important as visualisation is to achieving our goals, having faith that we WILL get there is crucial. At the outset of any journey, it's normal to have doubts about your success. Whenever those thoughts enter your mind, push those thoughts from your mind immediately. Those are your old habits talking, and a lifetime of scepticism won't disappear overnight. Maintaining your faith is something you'll need to practice every day. But the more you practise it, the quicker and more natural it will become. Again, it's turning your lightsabre from the dark side, using your force for good, and gripping that green lightsabre as you step forward into your new life.

Why *wouldn't* you have faith? With the timeline in Chapter 15, you've planned out every step of your brick-by-brick mission. It's just a matter of following your blueprint for success and you WILL get there. So whenever doubts creep into your mind, be confident in your plan and replace those doubts immediately with faith.

Now. Ready to dig in? Let's get down to business. Get out a pencil and paper and start writing out YOUR daily planner. Be crazy like Benny! You'll want to include:

- **Your goals!** Spend a chunk of time each day working towards your goals, whether that's study, work experience, research or networking.
- **Work**: even if you're trying to escape, that income is important to live on until your goal is achieved.
- **A sleep schedule:** bed time and wake up time, always allocating enough sleep to perform well.
- **Nutritious meals:** list all meals and ingredients so you can plan ahead when shopping.
- **Exercise!** Include it *no matter what.*
- **Socialising**: keep in touch with friends and family—even if it's a quick phone call, email or message.
- **A plan for procrastination!** Know the steps to act on if it arises so you can catch it, acknowledge it and then change course and keep moving forward.

The Happy Bricklayer
Mark Bayer

Deep thoughts for you to ponder:

- Remember, it takes only a fortnight to form new habits! Discipline will become easier as you start using your daily diary and allocating time towards each step.
- Get in the habit of quickly turning negative thoughts to positive ones. With practice, negative thoughts will arrive less and less because you are teaching your mind they are not necessary.
- Replace scepticism with Faith. You WILL get there!

The Happy Bricklayer
Mark Bayer

BRICK SIXTEEN: Do It Today, Not Tomorrow

What tasks have you procrastinated on before?
Have you planned your daily planner in detail?

The Happy Bricklayer
Mark Bayer

Does your daily planner include deadlines and a timeline?

Could you add some more detail into your planner?

The Happy Bricklayer
Mark Bayer

How long did you take to read this book after you got it?

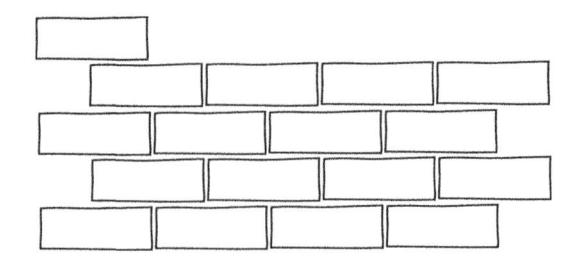

17. Communication

I heard a great story many years ago, told by a Dutch bricklayer. He immigrated to Australia in the late sixties, when Sydney was having a huge building boom, and he found construction work on a high-rise in the CBD, along with lots of other immigrants.

On this particular day, he was finishing up a lift shaft on the 30th floor when the foreman sent a new bricklayer up to join the crew. This new Greek guy was, as they say, fresh off the boat. He didn't speak a word of English.

Once they finished the job, they were supposed to head down a few levels and join the main crew of workers. As best he could, the Dutch guy instructed the new Greek guy to stay behind and "hose the snots," or clean the mortar off the back of the wall by leaning into the lift shaft and blasting it with a hose. Then he left the guy alone to finish the job.

Twenty minutes later, he heard someone yelling. It was coming from up on the top level. "BLUDGER!" someone was

The Happy Bricklayer
Mark Bayer

shouting. "BLUDGER, BLUDGER!" *Who the hell is calling out "bludger" like that?* No one could work out what was going on until he recognized the voice with the Greek accent. *That's strange,* the Dutch guy thought. *Why's he upstairs alone screaming "bludger?"* So he and a few others went up check what was going on.

Well lo and behold, the Greek guy had fallen head-first into the lift shaft and was tangled in the safety netting inside like a fly in a spider's web. His feet were in the air and he was just stuck there, screaming "BLUDGER, BLUDGER" in his Greek accent. They felt terrible for the poor guy—and at the same time, it was a hysterical thing to witness.

They hauled him up, and managed to work out that the only English word he could remember was "bludger." The Greek guy had no idea what it meant, but it was the only English word he could think of so he used that to call for help.

After that, I'm sure he started working on his English!

And I'm telling you this story of the unlucky Greek guy because really, it's all about COMMUNICATION. Communication is so important in all of your relationships. If you're planning to make big changes in your life, you've got to discuss them thoroughly with your loved ones, or anyone those changes will affect. If like me you want to take time off from work, how will that affect your family? Can you financially afford to do it? Will your employer let you reduce

The Happy Bricklayer
Mark Bayer

your hours? Will you still have time for your children and all their commitments?

Before you can design your brick-by-brick plan, you must be sure that everyone in your life is supportive.

My wife has been my biggest support person on this journey. It's funny, if I'm perfectly honest she has zero interest in my writing. Many times, I have asked for her feedback and she puts off reading my work for ages. Nevertheless, she sees how important writing is to me and how frustrated I became as a bricklayer and a builder. Luckily, she enjoys the variety in her work, and she's happy to continue full time whilst I live out my dream of becoming a writer. We've discussed this in depth and I'm sure she doesn't have any secret bitterness about my plan. Apart from squeezing a bit more housework out of me, she's glad to see me happy.

Fortunately, I have my own business, so I get to set my own schedule. I try and do smaller construction jobs these days, and if it's a bigger job I give myself a break when it's finished to work on my writing.

I also talk about my plans with my children. I want my kids to understand that finding satisfaction in your work life is just as important as providing for your family. If I were to continue in a job that was making me miserable, then I'd be bringing that negative

The Happy Bricklayer
Mark Bayer

energy home with me. I'd be short tempered, and using food and alcohol for comfort.

I explain to my children that they should be studying the subjects in school that they enjoy and find interesting—not the ones they hate but think they "should" study. "Listen to your heart and follow your passion," I tell them. (It's possible this has backfired: my 11-year-old is now hoping there's a gaming class in high school.)

Keep your communication open throughout your journey, and make sure everyone is on board as you progress. Your friends may be affected too, and they're a great source of honest feedback.

Want to hear another story about communication going wrong?

Many years ago, I was working as a bricklayer in London. The foreman was a cockney fella called Terry, and we had several laborers from Poland working with us at the time too.
One of the Polish guys was called Zippy. He was a great worker, but he hardly spoke a word of English.

One day we were pouring concrete into these large footings, and we needed a tool called a vibrator, which is not what you think it is but is actually used to shake the wet concrete so it fills any voids.

"Zippy! Go grab the vibrator," Terry screamed. Zippy took off as the concrete continued to flow. We waited: one minute, two, then three. Zippy wasn't back yet.

The Happy Bricklayer
Mark Bayer

At this point, Terry was stressing. "Where the fuck is Zippy with that bloody vibrator?" he hollered, and the other guys started yelling for Zippy.

Finally, back comes Zippy looking red and flustered, but instead of bringing the vibrator he hands Terry a cup of tea.

"WHAT THE FUCK IS THIS?" Terry wanted to know. We were all pissing ourselves laughing as the other Polish guys explained to Zippy what he'd done wrong. Zippy promptly went to get the vibrator, but I laugh every time I think of Zippy standing next to the kettle, urging it to boil faster as Terry screamed for him to hurry up.

You see the chaos that can happen when we don't communicate? Just like on a building site, life can get problematic if you don't keep your dialogue open and honest—especially when you're making such drastic changes in your life. Luckily, I don't think your loved ones will have as much trouble understanding you as Zippy did with that damned vibrator.

You should also be on the lookout for signs of discontent with the people in your life, even after they've agreed to changes. It's common for people to hide their true feelings and say they're okay, when really they're not.

For example, imagine you've cut your hours back at work to concentrate on your new goal. Your boss has agreed, and you're excited to get started. But maybe that's affected a colleague by

The Happy Bricklayer
Mark Bayer

placing more work on them. Or maybe you've stopped spending as much time with a friend as you used to, and that person might feel a little hurt.

Things might seem fine on the surface, but your life change might affect more than just your immediate family—so be aware, looks can be deceiving.

I was once deceived on a building site.

I'd hired my brother to work for me since he was saving up to go to Europe, and just like me, he's a big prankster. One day we were doing the brickwork for a project home. I was working on the front of the house, standing on some scaffold around two metres off the ground. Nearby was the Portaloo.

I noticed my brother go into the loo, and I knew he'd been in there more time than it takes to do a wee. So I did what any loving brother would do: I chucked a small piece of brick at the Portaloo, making a loud bang. I knew he'd be terrified, but at least he was in the right place to get a fright!

Smiling away I continued with my work, and after a few minutes the door flew open and my brother came racing out at me holding toilet paper smeared with dark brown stuff. Before I could react, he leaped up on the scaffold and smeared it on my bare leg.

Once I realised what he'd smeared on me, I went off my head. "You *dirty fucking bastard*," I muttered, climbing off the scaffold to

The Happy Bricklayer
Mark Bayer

chase him. He ran away, but as I gave chase he held up a jar of Vegemite. That's when I got it: he'd planned the whole thing. Knowing I couldn't resist throwing something at the Portaloo, he'd scooped some Vegemite onto the toilet paper and got me—hook, line and sinker!

(Actually, that's not at all the same deception you might experience on your journey, but couldn't resist sharing that story.)

Deep thoughts for you to ponder:

- Making big changes to your life could affect your family and friends.
- Discuss your plans with those affected before making big decisions.
- Feelings can change, so keep the lines of communication open.
- Be on the lookout for non-verbal signs of discontent.

Remember, if it looks like shit, smells like shit and tastes like shit. It's either shit, or vegemite.

The Happy Bricklayer
Mark Bayer

BRICK SEVENTEEN: The People Around You

Which people in your life will be affected by your changes?
What do you think their concerns may be?

The Happy Bricklayer
Mark Bayer

Do you think they may be reluctant to communicate their concerns to you?

Can you explain how your life changes could positively impact them?

The Happy Bricklayer
Mark Bayer

Do you like to eat Vegemite in a Portaloo?

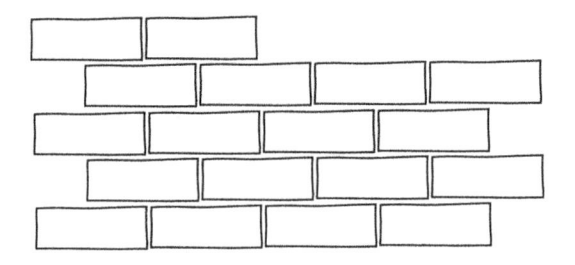

18. Work Balance

Writing a book takes a huge amount of time, and completing this one will be such a satisfying achievement for me. I hope it becomes popular, but finishing the manuscript alone will be a massive accomplishment. And the only way I've been able to dedicate enough time to writing is by not working full-time.

Right now, you could say I have two part-time jobs: building and writing. It helps that the two jobs are very different. When I studied life coaching, I discovered that a lot of people didn't necessarily despise their jobs; they just found them too monotonous. I believe that society in general would be much better off if we ALL had two part-time jobs to break up our week and add a little variety.

Can you imagine two days a week as a hairdresser and three days a week as a teacher? Or a florist and a policeman? A lawyer and a scuba dive instructor? To be perfectly honest, I can't believe it's not a more popular idea. One job that's a bit physical, one that's

The Happy Bricklayer
Mark Bayer

working with people, one that's creative, or a job with animals. If we started out our careers this way we'd be less inclined to feel bitter towards our jobs. Plus, with two skills, if you really ended up unhappy in one position, you could do the other full-time until you trained for a better third job!

For me, by averaging a good 15 to 20 hours a week writing, I'm able to progress my writing projects a lot faster than before. I enjoy the feeling of creativity, but I still use my years of experience to provide some income, and I don't feel so glum whilst doing it.

That's the biggest gold nugget I can offer you from my experience. If you can take that leap of faith and work part-time on your dream, I know you won't regret it—no matter the sacrifices you have to make. What have you got to lose? Go ahead and jump; it's less risky than staying miserable.

You might even start by trying it short-term. Do you have any holiday pay accrued in your job? Maybe you have eight weeks, or 40 days leave coming to you. If you take it part time, you could work a three days a week for 20 weeks straight. That's almost half a year you could dedicate to your dream life! You could spend it studying a new qualification, practicing a new skill, or creating pieces of art. You could even be learn to become a bricklayer!

At the end of those 20 weeks, you'll know what your next step will be. Maybe you'll make it a permanent thing and change

The Happy Bricklayer
Mark Bayer

your job—anything is possible! But you will have made a start on your path to happiness—and I GUARANTEE you will feel better than before.

So. What's holding you back?

If you're like I was, you've heard a lot of this information already—and yet you're still hesitating. There are plenty of excuses we tell ourselves. *The timing isn't right*, or *I can't be so selfish*. At some point you just have to take the risk.

But if you're still procrastinating, why not at least make a plan?

That's something I'm sure you can find the time to do. Work out exactly what you want your life to look like. Then, as we discussed in Chapters 15 and 16, work out your brick-by-brick strategy to achieve it. It might take you a few weeks, or even months to define it.

But I promise you this: if you have a clear and exact program that will take you from where you are now to living your dream life, you will feel a lot more positive about taking a leap of faith. In fact, it won't feel like a leap at all. Did you know our minds will not offer up any suggestions that we are not willing to undertake? That's a huge part of life coaching: the coach must *extract* the answers from their client—not suggest them—as we will not come up with steps that we are not willing to do.

The Happy Bricklayer
Mark Bayer

For example, when their client is trying to brainstorm ideas to drop 20kg, a life coach will first change their goal to a positive one: instead of saying "I wish to lose," they're encouraged to say "I wish to weigh." And if the goal is to lose weight, the last thing the life coach will do is suggest they train for a marathon. What if they hate everything about that idea? Much more effective is to ask the client what THEY think they could do to achieve their ideal weight. The client might come up with a surprising solution, like changing to a vegan diet and walking four days a week. That's a little bit of life coaching wisdom for you: when creating our own solutions, psychologically we have a much higher chance of success.

By the time you've worked out every final detail of your plan, guess what? You will already have begun your journey already, and laid the first bricks in your foundation of a happy life. You will have decided exactly how much time you are comfortable allocating towards your goal and you won't undertake a work life balance that doesn't satisfy all your family, financial and lifestyle commitments.

The Happy Bricklayer
Mark Bayer

> ## Deep thoughts for you to ponder:
>
> - Everyone has their own work life balance that they can commit to.
> - If you are unsure you can spare any time, at least make a detailed plan so you know exactly what it will take to achieve.
> - Use your holiday time to work on your goal—it will be as refreshing as a getaway.
> - Make sure YOU think up the steps! We only come up with ideas we're willing to do.

Bricklayers are not renowned for their balance, especially after a few beers at the pub on a Friday afternoon.

BRICK EIGHTEEN: Only So Many Hours In a Day

How much time per day can you allocate towards achieving your goals? How much is that per week? Per month?
What is the work-life balance you would like if money wasn't an issue?

The Happy Bricklayer
Mark Bayer

> How many beers can a bricklayer drink before he loses balance?

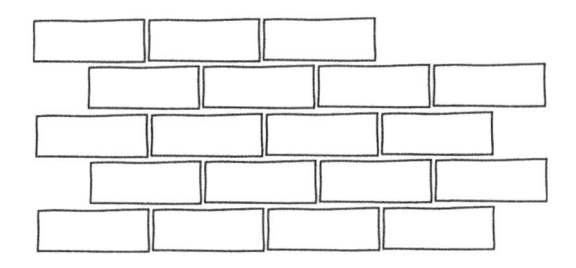

19. Inspiring Others

Over the years I have shared all my failures (and now my successes!) with my closest friends. We all have a number of people that we socialise with regularly, and these people become part of our "Village." We learn about each other's struggles over the years, and we share one another's ups and downs. All of my closest friends and family have all noticed huge changes in me these past few years.

I always had a reputation of being a hard worker: for decades I put in long hours at work on my own business, building my own homes in my spare time and making a lot of sacrifices.

But now I'm doing the opposite. I work part time, and from one point of view I look semi-retired. Of course, the truth is I'm working plenty of hours, just writing instead of building. When discussing this transformation with friends, I've found myself explaining my reasons in detail. Some people aren't interested, and who can blame them? I probably sound like a preacher, trying to convince them to join my new "Happy Bricklayer Cult." But I've

The Happy Bricklayer
Mark Bayer

noticed that some people just dismiss the thought of chasing one's dreams as unrealistic. Those stubborn buggers will just push on in their unhappy jobs 'till they're 65— and they don't want to discuss it, full stop.

It's not my business to force my opinions on anyone else, so I don't ram my ideas down anyone's throat. But some of my friends have seen me change, and they want to know more about how I'm doing it. I'm happy to share with them my story! Inspiring others to invest in themselves and seeing their improvements has been such a satisfying experience.

My friend Graeme is a school teacher and his dream job is to turn his side hustle into a full-time business. He writes people's biographies for them, with a printed book with their stories and photos, and an online version with the book and audio book read by the biographer, it's called People Pages. He has such passion for his work because it's entirely his own creation. At the moment though, he's a full-time teacher and has a wife, three kids, and another side gig playing drums in several local bands. His biography business gives him heaps of satisfaction, but he has barely a few hours left over at the end of the month to dedicate towards it.

So Graeme formulated a plan. Next year, he's leaving his fulltime role as a teacher and he believes he can survive on three days a week as a casual teacher.

The Happy Bricklayer
Mark Bayer

The hourly rate as a casual is higher, and it also frees up time in the evenings as he doesn't need to plan daily lessons like he does now. He'll be able to work two full days a week on his business, and his income will only drop slightly. He knows he will find teaching a lot more enjoyable when he doesn't spend his evenings planning lessons, and he'll have four days a week away from the classroom. He'll also be earning income from his biographies, and as his business expands he could choose to work more days on his business and fewer on teaching, but he'll have the freedom to choose what best suits him.

What a brilliant plan, and really simple to put in place and achieve.

Karl's another mate of mine, and he says I've inspired him to start on his journey to a happier life. His change has been a bit different, because his problem wasn't his career. He's an electrician, and he quite enjoys his work most of the time. But he just wasn't living his dream life. We had a chat about how I turned my life around, but he honestly had no other career aspirations—he just had issues with some parts of his job. I decided we would make a list of pros and cons:

The Happy Bricklayer
Mark Bayer

Being a Sydney Sparky

PROS	CONS
• Commercial jobs—big projects are way more interesting	• Driving in Sydney peak hour traffic
• Team environment with a good group of lads	• Climbing in roofs and under floors in residential
• Overtime opportunities	• Low pay on residential jobs

Once we laid it out like that, it was easy to see Karl had no real issues with his career—it was more the individual projects he was working on. Pretty much every job he had involved a long commute. He felt like residential work was a young man's game, physically demanding and offered little mental challenge and stimulation, so commercial was definitely his preference—but there wasn't a lot of commercial work in Sydney. Money was also a huge motivation for Karl. He had recently finished a large extension on his home and his wife didn't work, so he was the only provider for the family. Karl had previously worked on mining projects all around Australia, but those jobs had kept him away from home for a month

The Happy Bricklayer
Mark Bayer

at a time, and when he and his wife started a family he'd decided it was too hard being away that long.

But when Karl talked about those mining jobs, he liked everything else about it. He liked the work more than any other job; they worked longer hours and earned hardship pay so his wages were huge.

"Why can't you look for a mining job again, one that has shorter stints away from home?" I suggested. Karl thought his wife and daughter wouldn't allow it, even though he would be willing to try it.

"If you don't ask, you won't know," I told him.

A few days later, he called me up. "Guess what, I've got a new job!"

"Really?! Tell me all about it!"

Turns out, Karl did take it up with his family. And together, they discovered there were plenty of jobs where you were away for two weeks then home for one. With all the overtime he would double his income, doing the very work he enjoyed the most. Seeing how tired he was working in Sydney and driving in traffic, his wife thought he should give it a go. They could video call every day, and when he was home he would be there for a whole week. Just like that, Karl found a balance that's working for him and his family. The extra income is helping pay for the new extension on their home,

The Happy Bricklayer
Mark Bayer

and Karl is lucky enough to be working with a great bunch of guys—so working away from his loved ones is a whole lot easier. Not to mention, those lads like a beer as much as Karl does!

By searching for a position that ticked most of his boxes, Karl improved his life dramatically. That might not work for others but it works for him and his family. What's most important is to stop putting up with things that aren't satisfying you. Make a change. There might not be a job out there that is 100% perfect, but finding one that's pretty close is the next best thing.

What I learned from Karl is that sometimes it's not your job that is stopping you from being happy, it's your work environment. If that sounds like you, it's time to act and look for another position. Do you hate your commute? Perhaps you could work remotely some days, or look for a position closer to home. Maybe you can't stand your co-workers, and a change might help you find a better working environment that helps you enjoy your job again.

Whatever the reason you're dissatisfied, I know one thing for sure: doing nothing will mean you will continue in misery. So start looking around! It costs you nothing to apply for new positions—what have you got to lose?

The Happy Bricklayer
Mark Bayer

> ## Deep thoughts for you to ponder:
>
> - Find someone who is successful in your chosen career and use them for inspiration.
> - As you transform your life, you closest friends will notice. So, share your secret to success!
> - Don't force your new-found success on people though—only share if asked.

If you and your spouse are both working from home and haven't killed each other, you should consider writing a book on relationships.

The Happy Bricklayer
Mark Bayer

BRICK NINETEEN: Finding Inspiration

Who inspires you?

Who is living the life you wish to live?

The Happy Bricklayer
Mark Bayer

Who can you inspire to change their lives for the better?

What will be the things that have changed to make you feel you are achieving your goals?

The Happy Bricklayer
Mark Bayer

> What inspires you more? A bricklayer becoming an author, or a vegan keeping to themselves that they are a vegan?

The Happy Bricklayer
Mark Bayer

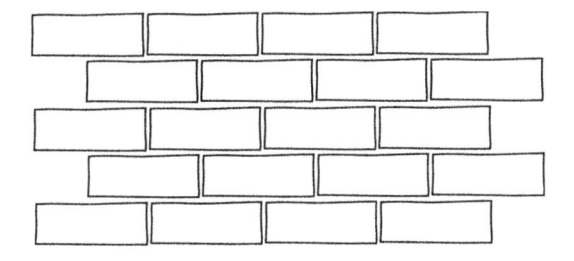

20. Multiskilled

Another advantage you will find when you are working in your new profession is that you now have two different skills. When I started on my journey many years ago, I would fantasize about the day I could throw my trowel away and never set eyes on a brick again. I was overworked and yearning for mental stimulation.

Years later, I decided that once I was financially secure with a passive income, I could give the bricklaying up forever to concentrate on being a writer full time. Now I'm not so sure. You see, I definitely prefer being a writer to a bricklayer, but I'm not convinced that doing any job exclusively is the best way to go.

When I started writing, my goal was to give up bricklaying, sell my movie scripts to Hollywood and become a bestselling author. I still want to achieve writing success, but giving up construction work completely would deny me some great experiences.

After working physically for almost 30 years, I'm strong and reasonably fit. Stopping physical work completely might not be great

The Happy Bricklayer
Mark Bayer

for my health. There's a certain pride I get from construction that I would miss. I've met some amazing characters on site, hilarious guys to have a laugh with—whereas when I'm a writer, I spend my days mostly alone. Then there's the instant financial reward that I get from construction (well, not instant with *some* clients) that writing doesn't give me. Most of my funniest anecdotes come from the array of characters I have met on building sites the last 30 years, maybe if I'd tried writing earlier I wouldn't have as many experiences to draw upon.

But the biggest change I have discovered on my journey has been my change of feeling towards by bricklaying work. To be honest it's been an absolute revelation. I was hopeful that I would become happier on the day's I was writing but figured I would still be a bit miserable on my bricklaying days. Incredibly after only a few months of part time work I have actually started to enjoy my building work for the first time in decades. The last time I enjoyed building work was ten years ago when building my own home. And I put that down to the creative side of designing and building my own home, creating exactly what I wanted instead of someone else's ideas, I never thought I could enjoy bricklaying for others but here I am excited about work. It's a pretty incredible and unexpected result.

You see when I was doing 40 to 50 hours of repetition for decades I was basically denying my sense of purpose, that creativity

The Happy Bricklayer
Mark Bayer

that I get from writing. But now I am able to scratch that itch, regularly, I wake up with a spring in my step. Even when driving in Sydney traffic to construction sites, I am excited as I am able to feel positive about bringing in some income, satisfying clients by building things for them and I am able to use my imagination to plan writing ideas and know that in only a short time I will be back at my keyboard moving forward with my book and scripts. I have completely lost that feeling of dread going to work. I had no idea that I would feel like this, I have realised my goal already of living my dream life, because I am now "The Happy Bricklayer". Being a published author, and selling movie scripts to Hollywood will be amazing when they happen in the future but those goals were what I thought it would take to make me feel happy, when in fact just working on those goals gives me the same feeling of satisfaction, and appreciation for my bricklaying work.

You see, as I've moved along my journey, I've had to adapt and re-evaluate my goal. I now realise that happiness comes from getting the balance right—and zero percent bricklaying would actually be a bad thing for me. Now I'm currently adjusting my goal: at the moment, I feel an 80/20 balance sounds good. I'll write most days, and every couple of weeks I'll spend a couple of days on site, chatting with the boys and slapping in a few bricks. That ratio is a work in progress—but being on the path feels as good as achieving

The Happy Bricklayer
Mark Bayer

my dream. That's why it's so important for you to get started, because in such a short peiod of time you will be able to feeling like me, happy and satisfied and you don't need to achieve the end goal to have that feeling, the journey there feels just as good.

As time goes on I have the luxury of choosing my balance, and I'm open to the possibility that my feelings may change over time. That's fine— this isn't something we ever finish striving for. Finding a harmonious balance in our lives will be an ever-changing challenge, but it excites me—and I guarantee it will excite you, too.

Deep thoughts for you to ponder:

- Learning a new skill means you're less likely to get bored.
- Once you're working in your dream job, you'll find you no longer hate your old job.
- Having two different skills gives you the freedom to choose the best balance for you.

Maybe they were wrong, it is possible to have your cake and eat it too!

The Happy Bricklayer
Mark Bayer

BRICK TWENTY: Finding Your Best Balance

Describe the differences between your dream job and old job:
Do you plan on giving up your old job completely, or working part time between that and your new job?

The Happy Bricklayer
Mark Bayer

What ratio do you plan to balance between the two jobs?

What skills do the two jobs share?

The Happy Bricklayer
Mark Bayer

Are you able to tap on top of your head with one hand and rub circles on your belly with the other hand? Knew it, multi-talented already?

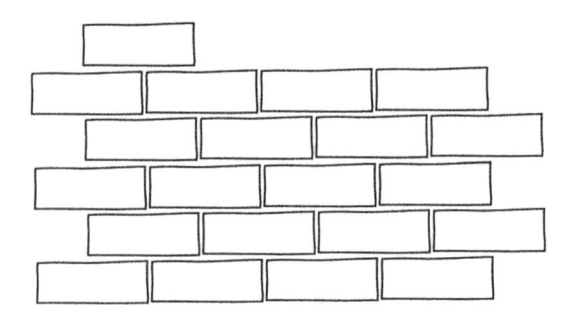

21. Chain Reaction

For anyone who's spent as long as I have yearning for a change, the hardest part is laying that first brick. If you can commit to taking that first step on your journey, you have actually done the hardest part—and unfortunately, it's a step that many won't take. I can promise you though, once you start building your dream life the amazing feelings you get will start to snowball. No one told me this—it's something I discovered along the way. If I had known that it got easier and more exciting with each brick I laid to build my dream life, I definitely would have started much sooner.

From the moment I made the commitment to myself after my hypnotherapy session with Lauren, I haven't looked back. Sometimes, you just need an outside voice to get a little clarity.

During our session way back then, Lauren asked me about my first day on a building site. How did I perform? Was I competent?

The Happy Bricklayer
Mark Bayer

"Nope," I told her. "Actually I was a 17-year-old chubby, pimply boy on a building site and I really struggled. I wasn't strong, and it was hot, and I pushed wheelbarrows full of bricks, and I even dropped a wheelbarrow full of mortar on the ground. I was exhausted and I couldn't keep up."

Lauren nodded. "Fair to say you started poorly. And how about now? Are you a good bricklayer?"

"Well of course," I said, trying not to sound like a twat. "Now I'm at the top of my trade. I'm extremely fast and neat, I've worked on all kinds of projects here and in London, completing all kinds of fancy arches and difficult work, I've been a foreman and I've run my own business. I'm in the top few percent of tradesman, I'd say."

"So why can't you do the same with writing?" she asked.

Whack, that felt like a slap in the face with a dead fish.

Of course, she was perfectly right. Sure, I might not be an acclaimed author straight away, but if I work at improving and I keep at it, history has shown that I rise to the top.

"If you hated bricklaying and you *still* rose to the top," Lauren continued, "imagine what you can achieve with writing, since it's what you love."

From that day forward, I transformed. And as time goes on, I've noticed a chain reaction. The time spent writing brings me joy. Hey, it's not always easy. Some days I struggle, but generally I'm

The Happy Bricklayer
Mark Bayer

satisfied creating characters on the page and telling stories. With satisfying my creative side I am no longer looking to food for short term gratification. Having gained control of my diet, I am fit and slimmer, which brings me more confidence and improves my relationships with the people around me. I have more energy for the gym and training for my half-marathons, and racing gives me an incredible sense of accomplishment.

All of these positive things are happening and I'm only part way through building my dream life! I wake up each morning with a new zest for the day. Construction no longer makes me feel anxious, and I don't dread it. When I'm on a building site, I'm always looking forward to my next writing day, and that makes work easier to tolerate. I don't have so many aches and pains because I have plenty of days off the tools, but I'm still keeping strong and work fit. Then I have plenty of energy left over for my writing day, when I work long hours to get the most out of them.

However, it took me a little while to find a schedule to my new working life, especially with my writing. When I write, I need peace and no interruptions. I struggle to get much writing done on weekends when the family's around, or on weeknights with kids' sport and socialising. In my first few days of writing I would wake with no alarm; the alarm used to represent a job I despised so that sound was extremely negative to me. I woke up later with the family,

The Happy Bricklayer
Mark Bayer

chilled out whilst they got ready and when they all left for school and work I would head to the gym. Exercise, home for a shower, breakfast and ready to write. The problem with that was, I barely got four hours of writing in before the kids were home from school. How was I going to fit in a full eight-hour day?

Very quickly, I decided that I had to start exercising before 7 AM or after 4 PM. At first, I thought that would be a nightmare, because I always dreaded waking up early for bricklaying. But to my surprise, I no longer hate early starts. I used to wake with as much enthusiasm as an old, arthritic, overweight dog chasing a ball. But when waking up for a run at the gym I'm excited. I'm at the gym from 6-7 AM and I enjoy running on a treadmill—for me, it works because I'm able to multi task. I get my exercise in and watch sport on my phone. Even if you prefer exercising outside, you can multi task with earphones and listen to music, or books and podcasts. This can help to free up time you can put towards working on your goal. You can learn new information as you listen to lessons whilst exercising.

After the gym, I get home to have breakfast with my family, keeping in touch with their schoolwork, sports, hobbies, and friendships. Once they head out the door, I'm immediately in my study, on the keyboard, writing for a solid seven hours without interruption. By starting my day sooner, I was able to nearly double my writing time. Plus, I'm already caught up on the sports results!

The Happy Bricklayer
Mark Bayer

Back to the chain reaction! It feels like every aspect of my life has improved, and I'm only part way on my journey to achieving my goal. Sure, reaching the goal you are striving for will give you a feeling of happiness and contentment, but *you can have that same feeling along the way.* Each day, as you add a brick to your dream build, you will already have the feeling of happiness that you're striving for. And that will be a cycle you will continue all the way to achieving your dream life. The whole reason we want to change our work life is to be happier, but I can't reinforce enough how you will already be happy as you begin your dream build and start adding bricks to your dream life, the end result will be a fantastic achievement, but the journey itself will make every day enjoyable.

The Happy Bricklayer
Mark Bayer

Deep thoughts for you to ponder:

- Every single day you lay a brick on your dream life build, you will get a feeling of achievement.
- Taking daily steps towards your goal builds unstoppable momentum.
- You can always adjust your plans as you learn what works and doesn't.
- Habits form quickly! Hitting your targets every day will become your new routine.
- Meeting daily goals is hugely satisfying, and it will start a chain reaction that will bring positivity to all areas of your life.

Your progress is like a snowball at the top of a snow-covered hill, as it accelerates and grows and rolls down the hill, try to avoid any patches of yellow snow

The Happy Bricklayer
Mark Bayer

BRICK TWENTY-ONE: The Snowball Effect

How will you feel when you lay your first brick from your detailed blue print to success?

What aspects of your life will improve as you keep moving towards your goal?

The Happy Bricklayer
Mark Bayer

What new habits will you form on your journey to a new life?

What would the title of your autobiography be?

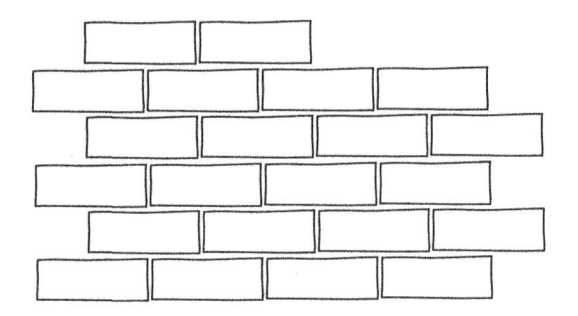

22. Self-Help Resources

I love non-fiction self-improvement books. Each one I've read has given me a useful tool or inspired me in some way. I believe the greatest thing we can do with our lives is to continually improve ourselves by learning new ways to achieve our dreams. One of the gripes I have had over the years is that some self-help books tend to focus on one main idea and then repeat themselves, making them tough to read. We're all individuals, and what works for some won't work for others. For that reason, I'd like to describe multiple tools—some worked for me, and some ideas worked for others. There are so many resources that can help you achieve your goals and you need to discover the tools that fit your unique situation. Once you've settled on your goal, the next step is brainstorming ways of achieving your goal. No idea is a bad idea! By thinking outside of the box, you might discover a new technique that works for you—because let's face it, the old ideas haven't worked yet.

The Happy Bricklayer
Mark Bayer

Manifesting

Manifesting is based on the idea that you can think your dreams into reality. By focusing on a precise vision, you can attract your dream into your life. It is also known as the law of attraction. There's a reason that books written on this topic are some of the biggest selling nonfiction books on the market: it really works. For me I go to bed every night visualizing my future life. I see myself as a published author, having meetings with editors and agents, travelling overseas and selling movie scripts in Hollywood.

I have a note on my study wall that I read aloud every day when I write. It details the same thing: my goal of becoming a successful writer. I am definitely closer to achieving this dream than I was when I started. Thanks to you also for reading this book and helping me achieve my dream! Hopefully I've inspired you to reach yours.

Manifesting includes the belief that your mind cannot distinguish the difference between what you see with your eyes and what you see in your imagination. If you keep presenting your mind with images of where you want to be, your subconscious will formulate a way of achieving your goals. The more time you spend manifesting your goals, the better results you will achieve.

Manifesting has a very low bar to entry: it costs nothing and can be done regularly. without taking up much of your schedule.

The Happy Bricklayer
Mark Bayer

Meditation

Probably the oldest technique for bringing a calm balance to your life, meditation has been used for thousands of years, all over the world. It helps to clear the information overload that builds up and can overwhelm us. It can wipe away stress and anxiety, and help you find inner peace—a feeling that can last long after you've finished your session.

Meditation takes some practise. There are classes everywhere, plus there are heaps of online options that vary in length and philosophical approach.

Starting or finishing your day with meditation can really help you stay in the right frame of mind to continue adding bricks to your dream life build.

Breathing

Trying new breathing techniques can be a great option to help relax and calm yourself, or to help you focus and concentrate. There are lots of different approaches to conscious breathing. I learned the "box breathing technique" from a psychologist to help me with anxiety. It only takes a minute, and you can repeat it as long as you want. If you get dizzy, just stop until you feel okay, then and start again. Little by little, you will improve.

The Happy Bricklayer
Mark Bayer

Close your eyes and imagine a square. Breathe in slowly through your nose and feel the air enter your lungs as you move along one side of the square in your mind. Hold your breath for four seconds. Slowly exhale through your mouth for four seconds. Then repeat for the other 3 sides of the square.

The box breathing technique is just one of many—have a Google and you will find plenty online.

Cold Water Therapy

Have you ever had a cold shower? It isn't a pleasant sensation! It's a shock to our system. Nonetheless it has huge benefits—and I suggest you give it a try.

If you sometimes deal with anxiety, give it a go! Many people start their day with a cold shower, and I can tell you it's a thousand times better than a coffee. The shock of the cold water spikes your energy levels and improves circulation. It can also reduce inflammation, help you sleep better, improve alertness and concentration, improve your immune system, and reduce muscle soreness.

My first experiment with cold water therapy was at a gym. They had a steam room, a sauna, a big waterfall shower between them, and a crushed ice machine. After a workout I would go between the sauna and steam room for a few 5-minute sessions,

The Happy Bricklayer
Mark Bayer

then jump under the cold shower, rubbing handfuls of crushed ice over my body. It would literally take my breath away, it was so invigorating! Even the anticipation before jumping under the water got my heart racing, and afterwards I felt amazing.

It was years later that I learned about all the benefits of cold-water therapy, and these days I have a much simpler version: I splash cold water on my face first thing in the morning. That small act helps me stick to my goal because I'm instantly alert and ready to go. I hit the ground running—and it helps me to stop sitting on the toilet for 30 minutes, just looking at my phone!

Maybe you're lucky enough to live near the beach. If so, try and take a quick dip, any time of day. That adrenaline rush of diving into the water and shocking your system has so many benefits. I have even heard of some high achievers having a cold plunge pool at their homes, just for their daily therapy.

Yoga

Yoga is a real treat for the body. The older I get, working physically and running a lot, I find my muscles are constantly sore. I've never had the guts to try an actual yoga class at the gym. Firstly I'm not very flexible—but mainly I have zero confidence in completing those movements without farting.

The Happy Bricklayer
Mark Bayer

I do yoga at home with a free class on YouTube. Again, there are so many to choose from! You can find everything from a ten-minute whole-body class to an hour focussed just on your legs, plus hundreds of variations in between. If you haven't tried yoga, I promise you will feel better after. It helps with flexibility, and it can remove pain and soreness.

I had an Achilles injury a few years ago when I trained to run some marathons. I did zero stretching or yoga back then, and after I finished the marathon I saw a physio who suggested a few months off to let myself heal. Well, two years later and ten kilos heavier, I was finally able to run again. So far, I've avoided injury by stretching my legs with an online yoga lesson.

The best part of yoga is that stretching your muscles feels so good! Your whole body feels fantastic afterwards, and you'll be ready to take on the world. Give it a try.

Physical Activity

This one's a no brainer. A balanced life MUST include exercise. If you currently don't exercise, this should definitely be a part of your plans when designing your dream life. Exercise brings you so many benefits, both mental and physical, and the more you do the bigger the rewards. Believe me, I know how hard it is to get started—I used to struggle to get to the gym. I lifted weights back in

The Happy Bricklayer
Mark Bayer

my twenties, but it was always a struggle to find a friend to train with. Even then I would train hard, lifting huge weights, but I never slimmed down. My problem was that building muscle brings a huge appetite. And if you don't have a good knowledge of nutrition you end up eating the wrong foods.

Then I met Fran, a trainer at my gym in London. Fran was Spanish, ex special forces, and he was training to be an Iron Man. In short, Fran knew his shit.

Fran took me around the gym and asked me what my usual workout looked like. I showed him the weight routine I did and he stopped me and said, "No more weights. Mark, look how strong you are already! Big chest and arms, plus you're lifting bricks and heavy things all day at work! Today we start cardio."

It sounded like torture to me. Sure, I played lots of sport growing up, but fitness was never my best attribute.

Fran set me a simple goal at first: run one kilometre without stopping, then walk. Next it was run two kilometres without stopping then walk, and within a month I was able to run for an hour. That's how quickly I improved, and I've been addicted ever since. With Fran's help, I started running three to four times a week, and I and dropped 15 kilos in less than six months. I looked and felt great, my wife was pleased, and I had more confidence.

The Happy Bricklayer
Mark Bayer

So, if exercise has not been part of your life, change it. The positive feelings will help that chain reaction and snowball into other aspects of your life as you build towards your goal. If you need some help and you can't afford a personal trainer or even a gym membership, ask a friend. We all know someone who's super fit. Ask them for advice, tell them you're working towards your perfect life, and they'll surely love to help you achieve it. You can exercise anywhere, without any equipment. There are loads of free fitness classes online. It's just a matter of commitment. Make it happen.

Nutrition

Just as important, if not more important, than exercise is nutrition. Most of us are aware of what we should be eating, but we tend to get a bit slack. It's not easy, we're all super busy and it's difficult to have all the healthy ingredients on hand at all times. Plus, let's be honest—some of that junk food tastes so damn good. When you are looking to improve your life, nutrition can absolutely help. By having a close look at what you eat, you can make small changes that can have big effects.

Have you ever kept a food diary? It's a little frightening when you first do it. But if you commit to being truthful, it actually has an instant effect—motivating you to make better choices, as the diary will show the evidence. Not all of us have weight issues, but a healthy

The Happy Bricklayer
Mark Bayer

diet is important for brain function and energy levels as well. I used a nutritionist a few years back and found her very helpful, especially when it came to basic meal planning. Shop for specific ingredients, instead of just wandering the isles filling your basket with whatever catches your eyes. Meal planning will help you stick to your overall programme and give you the best chance of success. Oh, and never go shopping when you're hungry, either—it never ends well!

Therapy

Most of my success has come with the help of other people. It's not easy to go it alone, and having a professional to talk with can be a big help. If you can afford it, I suggest you find someone to help you work out what you want to do with your life. When I did life coaching, rarely did the person's goal at the beginning of a session remain the same by the end of the session.

Sometimes we can't see past our obstacles, but a therapist can. They do it every day.
The first therapist I saw helped me identify that I was looking for a change and that helped me to start up a new business. (Maybe I should get her to cough up the money I lost on that app, haha!) The next helped me with my grief after losing a dear friend. But the most success I had was with Lauren. Treating a problem is okay, but the reason behind the issue is just as important. Lauren was definitive in

her explanation, that writing is what I was born to do—and she helped me believe it was possible. If you don't know what you want to do with your life, but you know you aren't happy now, a therapist could help you find your sense of purpose.

If finances are tight, many therapists are subsidised by the government and you can usually get part of your costs covered with a referral from your GP. Even the government is aware of just how important mental health is, and therapy could be exactly what you need.

Sleep

A good night's sleep might be the most overlooked tool to improve our lives. I mentioned how I despised my alarm clock for decades, and how these days I love an early start and exercise, all before my working day begins. Back when I hated my job, I would stay up late, avoiding bed. I know I was unconsciously trying to delay the inevitable by staying awake longer. Then I'd wake up exhausted, yawning, and drowsy, headed out the door to a job I despised. Makes no sense—but that's what I was doing.

So much of our lives depends on a good night's sleep. Some of us need more sleep than others, but generally 6-8 hours is the recommended sleep for adults. Of course, when you're constantly

The Happy Bricklayer
Mark Bayer

denying yourself that, the vicious cycle begins and it's very hard to break.

When we're sleep deprived, our whole body is affected. Our immune system, blood pressure, stress hormones, breathing, appetite and cardiovascular health all suffer.

When I was surviving on 5 hours' sleep, I was waking tired, I had no energy, and I couldn't be bothered preparing a healthy lunch for work. Then I drank energy drinks to get me through the day, causing me to be overweight—and the spiral got worse and worse as time went on.

So when working on your blueprint, you HAVE to include a good night's sleep in your daily planner. The odd night out won't be an issue, but by setting a bedtime and sticking to it, you will guarantee you have the energy to add the bricks each day towards your dream build.

Of course these days, I'm happy to go to bed because I'm excited about the next day, and I know that with a good night's rest I'll have plenty of creative enthusiasm at the keyboard, and plenty of strength when slapping some bricks in at work.

The best part about sleep is that when you're happy and content, you need less of it. Being stressed or depressed takes a toll on your body, and you end up needing more sleep than normal.

The Happy Bricklayer
Mark Bayer

Positive and negative habits can both snowball—so make sure to prioritise a good night's sleep.

Deep thoughts for you to ponder:

- What works for one person might not work for another.
- Choose your own options, but make sure you know all the options available.
- Visualisation is the most popular tool in all self-help books.
- Make manifesting a habit to achieve your goals.
- Mental and Physical well-being are equally important.
- A good night's sleep is essential for your health and productivity.

Roses are red, Violets are blue, I finally got my shit together, now how about you do too

The Happy Bricklayer
Mark Bayer

BRICK TWENTY-TWO: Help Along The Way

Have you ever used any of the resources described in this chapter?
Which ones have you found helpful and why?

The Happy Bricklayer
Mark Bayer

Are you willing to try any new tools to help you reach your goals?

What self-improvement books have you read?

The Happy Bricklayer
Mark Bayer

What is your favourite one and why?

What are the biggest things you learned from those books?

The Happy Bricklayer
Mark Bayer

Have you bought a self-help book from an adult book store?

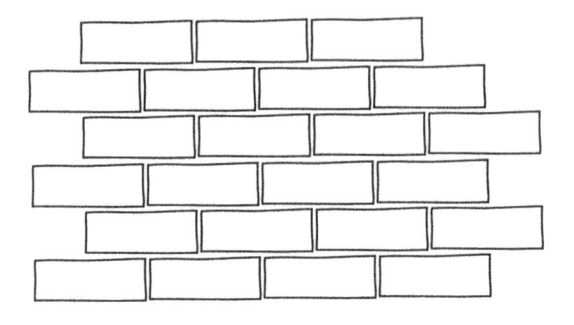

23. What's Holding You Back

You now have every tool at your disposal...but you're still procrastinating. You wouldn't have picked this book up if you were already living your dream life, so why not start now?

It is time to finally commit to yourself and take that leap of faith. If you don't change, you will continue feeling discontented, never quite satisfied or accomplished. We've all been conditioned to feel guilty or selfish for spending time and money on ourselves, but that's wrong.

Are you waiting for the right time? That may never come. You will adapt to your new schedule. I can guarantee it, because you won't make a plan that is unrealistic or doesn't fit with your values or the needs of your loved ones. So make the plan. Now IS the right time! There is absolutely nothing else as important than finding your happiness by living your dream life.

The Happy Bricklayer
Mark Bayer

That little voice in your head that's telling you all the reasons why you can't start? That pessimistic voice is your dark side. It's been holding you back for so long, and now it's time to take control by fighting back. Every time a negative thought or reason to give up arises, turn that red lightsabre into a green one. Think of a positive reason why you *should* proceed or why you *can* start. Think of all the amazing feelings you'll experience, not only when you reach your goal and have built your dream life, but with every brick you lay along the way. Each step will give you a sense of satisfaction and a feeling of pride for believing in yourself. The constant addition of these bricks will soon become addictive, and before you know it, those dark side red lightsabre moments will become fewer and fewer. Eventually, they won't be in control anymore—YOU will be.

You don't have to go it alone, either. This is definitely your journey and your life, but you can ask for help along the way. Talk with your closest friends and family, ask for help, and if necessary seek out a coach, therapist, mentor or psychologist. Those professionals are there to help people achieve their goals, and you don't need to be an egg short of an omelette to seek professional help. Some of their services are even subsidised by the government, at least in Australia. In any event, it doesn't cost anything to ask!

You don't need permission from anyone but yourself to make changes in your life, but good communication with the people

The Happy Bricklayer
Mark Bayer

around you is crucial. By being open and discussing your plans, you can compromise and find a schedule that works for everyone. Regular, open conversations along the way will stop any feelings of resentment or frustration, and you'll be able to adjust your blue print when challenges arise.

Fearing failure is normal, but we can easily move past that with careful planning. Remember—you've already gained a skill in your current job, so why can't you do it again? Especially if it's something you have a real passion for. Manage your expectations, and if it takes longer to achieve your goal then that's okay, because in the end you WILL achieve it.

Remember, building your dream life starts a chain reaction. When you no longer dread waking for work in the morning, you won't be starting your day with junk food, energy drinks or a cigarette. You will have gained control of your addictions, and not only will your work life be more satisfying but your health will improve. You will look and feel amazing, everyone will notice, and the positivity will snowball into every aspect of your life. You will waste less time on social media and TV, spend more time with loved ones, and improve all your relationships.

Focus on those images as often as you can. There's no way you won't make a start when you can see that amazing life ahead of you, especially with a clear, concise blue print and a daily planner

The Happy Bricklayer
Mark Bayer

showing every brick you need to lay each day on your way to building your dream life.

And what if all my aimless wanderings and idiot blunders actually resulted in some good advice? Well, if part of your journey has resulted in you becoming a kazillionaire, please send a cheque to the Happy Bricklayer (or maybe just buy a copy of this book for all your family and friends.)

Congratulations—YOU DID IT!
(Or at least, I feel confident you WILL do it soon.)

The Happy Bricklayer
Mark Bayer

BRICK TWENTY-THREE: Start Already!

What has held you back from starting before?

How will you overcome that this time?

The Happy Bricklayer
Mark Bayer

How will you feel if you never start?

How would you feel if you achieved your goal?

The Happy Bricklayer
Mark Bayer

Who can you ask to help you achieve your goal?

How important is it to you to achieve your goal?

The Happy Bricklayer
Mark Bayer

What celebrity would play you in a movie about your life?

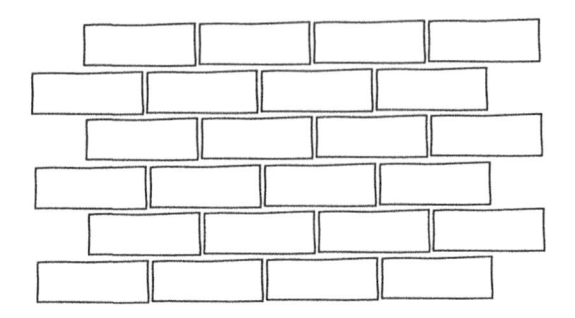

24. The Bricklayer's Blueprint For Success

By now, I'm sure you are ready to take that first step towards changing your life for the better. In fact, let's make that step two. Purchasing this book was your first step. You decided to invest in yourself, and that is the greatest investment any of us can make so *Bravo!*

In this chapter, we'll summarize what we've learnt so far, and use it towards the journey you're about to embark on. There are more questions to help you explore ideas and options, and help you draw up your brick by brick blueprint that will detail each and every step you will take to build your dream life. These questions are designed to help you decide what will work, what has held you back before, how to overcome obstacles, and exactly how long it will take to build your dream life.

The Happy Bricklayer
Mark Bayer

Step One

- Appreciate your job. Be thankful for what you do have. Sure, you want to make a change, but have you have been focusing too much on the negatives?
- Make a list of all the positives.
- What skills have you learned?
- Do you help others? What's best part of your job?
- Has your job helped you to provide for yourself and your family?
- Have you made any friends at work?
- In the short term, try and remember the good things about your job instead of just the negatives. This helps you have an immediate psychological improvement because you are focusing on the positives, not dwelling on the negatives, and you have started adding bricks to your dream life build.

Step Two

Do you know your sense of purpose? What do you feel you were put here on this earth for? What would you like to do with your life? If you want to change your life, you first have to work out what your sense of purpose is so you can then write down your goal. If you already know what you want, that's great. Most of us know what we don't want—it's a lot harder to decide what we DO want.

The Happy Bricklayer
Mark Bayer

An exercise that can really help in finding your sense of purpose is MIND MAPPING. Mind mapping is when you explore topics to get more ideas and options, opening up new and unthought-of opportunities. You can use mind maps for business plans, event planning, story writing, studying, and many other things.

Start with a blank piece of paper and draw a circle in the centre. Inside that circle, write the words "sense of purpose." Now draw lines coming away from it the circle, like spokes on a wheel or branches. At the end of each of those branches, draw another smaller circle and write different themes that are important to you. Some examples might be: *creativity, working with my hands, having a friendly work environment*, and so on. Once you've explored every branch and added new ones, you can repeat the exercise with a third series of branches. You might find a larger sheet of paper is necessary, and there are also many free mind mapping tools available online.

At the end of the exercise, you should have dozens if not hundreds of words describing the values that are most important to you. Explore each one, highlighting the most essential ones. With these ideas, you will hopefully settle on your sense of purpose. Once you've done that, you can try mind mapping careers that would satisfy your sense of purpose. Mind maps are a great tool to help brainstorming all sorts of possibilities. Remember it IS possible to make a living out of creative pursuits, think positive, you CAN achieve anything!

Step Three

You have your goal. Now, how will you achieve it? A new happy life doing a job you were born for. You need to design a plan with every detail of what it will take to make it happen. It will be difficult at times, and you will have to sacrifice, but I promise you the results will be worth it. Break your goal down into dozens of small, achievable steps. This will be your blueprint for a happy life. And you WILL make it a reality because YOU came up with it. You made all the decisions and you would only suggest things that you're willing to do—right? Each step you will be working towards each day, with your daily planner allocating time to achieve your targets. It is crucial that you spend a lot of time on your daily planner, if you can each day keep adding bricks onto your dream build, the walls will rise around you and the progress is steady and exciting. It takes thousands of little bricks to build that dream life, but each day you will see the progress and because you are following your exact blue print you are sure that it will become a reality.

How important is it to you to achieve your goal?

The Happy Bricklayer
Mark Bayer

>What obstacles are stopping you from achieving your goal?
>
>How will you overcome these obstacles?
>
>Who can help you achieve your goal?
>
>How realistic is your goal?
>
>How will achieving your goal impact other areas of your life?
>
>What would achieving your goal mean to you?
>
>What motivates you?
>
>How committed are you to the process of change?
>
>How much support do you have from family and friends?

Step Four

Visualise yourself living your ideal life. Start your day by closing your eyes and imagining what it looks like to live out your sense of purpose every day. How happy will you feel? How are your family and friends responding to you in this blissful state? Practice this several times a day, especially before sleep and straight after waking. Keep reinforcing these positive thoughts into your mind.

Remember, your brain can't distinguish the difference between what it sees through your eyes and what it sees in your imagination. By giving your brain regular glimpses of you living your dream life, you are allowing your subconscious mind to start plotting a way to make that life a reality.

The Happy Bricklayer
Mark Bayer

What will your life look like when you have achieved your goal?

What will success feel like?

What will your life look like in the next year? 3 years? 10 years?

Step Five

Follow your steps. Every day should be planned out. Remember, it takes a few weeks to form new habits—so it might be tough to stick it out at the beginning. Keep believing! By starting this journey you are already beginning to live your ideal life, and I'm sure you're already beginning to feel happier. Check in with yourself regularly. Don't forget to plan in chill out time, time with loved ones. Ask yourself: *If I win the lottery, what would I do with my days?* THAT's what you're working towards. It is extremely important you have a fixed time on achieving each and every milestone, without a time commitment you are giving yourself excuses to not complete your dream build.

How committed are you to making the necessary changes?

How open are you to trying new things?

What might get you off track?

How ill you get back on track?

The Happy Bricklayer
Mark Bayer

Step Six

Don't let setbacks deter you from achieving your dream. If you're not coping with your schedule, it just means you need to readjust it, and it might take a bit longer to get there. If you ruin your diet with a litre of ice cream, or if you skip a study session, it's not the end of the world, it's an opportunity to re-evaluate the plan and tweak it as you go.

A fear of failure can get into your mind and stop you from staying on target, but the REAL failure is to spend each day unhappy. If you dedicate enough time to your goals, eventually you will achieve everything you desire. Get in practise of acting fast on a negative thought, turn you red light sabre to a green one, replace negative thoughts with visions of you reaching your goals and feel that amazing sensation of what it will feel like when you WILL achieve it, it's only a matter of time as you are on your way.

How would overcoming obstacles make you feel?

How flexible are you in making necessary changes to achieve success?

Are you willing to do whatever it takes to achieve your goal?

The Happy Bricklayer
Mark Bayer

Step Seven

You've done it! You're living your dream life, every day has a sense of purpose and you're finally happy. You made the changes and you wake up each day with a smile.

Congratulations—YOU DID IT!

Printed in Great Britain
by Amazon